T0315970

THIS BOOK WILL TEACH YOU TO

START YOUR OWN BUSINESS

THE INSIDER'S GUIDE TO ENTREPRENEURSHIP

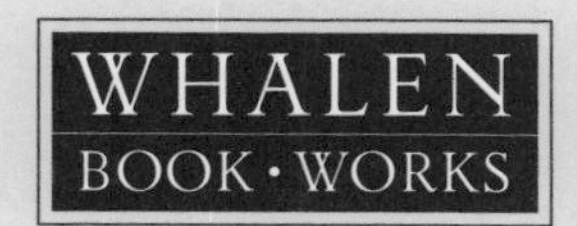

This Book Will Teach You to Start Your Own Business

13-digit ISBN: 978-1-95151-111-1
10-digit ISBN: 1-95151-111-1

This book may be ordered by mail from the publisher. Please include $5.99 for postage and handling. Please support your local bookseller first!

Books published by Whalen Book Works are available at special discounts when purchased in bulk. For more information, please email us at info@whalenbookworks.com.

Whalen Book Works
68 North Street
Kennebunkport, ME 04046

www.whalenbookworks.com

Printed in China
1 2 3 4 5 6 7 8 9 0

First Edition

"A BIG BUSINESS
STARTS SMALL."
—RICHARD BRANSON

CONTENTS

INTRODUCTION 6

CHAPTER 1: GETTING STARTED ON GOING IT ALONE 8

Eleven Qualities of the Entrepreneur's Mindset. 9

What Kind of Business Do You Want? Nine Questions to Ask 13

Ideas versus Opportunities: They're Not the Same Thing! 17

Brick and Mortar versus Online: The Pros and Cons of Each 20

A Sole Proprietor versus a Corporation: Which Is Right for You? 25

Going It Alone versus Having Partners 28

Crafting an Excellent Business Plan: Nine Essential Components 32

Eight Tips for Setting and Meeting Your Goals. 36

Stay at Your Job, or Quit and Boldly Forge Ahead on Your Own? (Hint: Stay at Your Job) 40

CHAPTER 2: NETWORKING: IT'S ALL ABOUT WHO YOU KNOW 43

Five Ways of Cultivating New Relationships 45

Your Network at Your Job: Five Actions to Take 48

Professional Networks. 51

Your Network in Your Personal Life: Nurturing Relationships with Those You Already Know 53

Networking Online with Social Media. 56

CHAPTER 3: MARKETING AND SELLING FOR YOURSELF: IT'S ALL ABOUT WHOM YOU REACH. 59

What Is Marketing? 60

Doing Market Research. 62

Finding the Right Market: Six Methods 65

Developing a Marketing Plan: Nine Steps. 68

Four Points for Creating a Marketing Budget 71

Creating Your Website: Seven Things to Remember 73

Marketing with Traditional Media 76

The Many Types of (Internet) Marketing 82

Marketing with Social Media 86

The Basics of Selling 90

Finding and Identifying Potential Customers 92

You've Got a Potential Customer, Now What? Six Suggestions 95

How to Close the Deal 97

Nine Ways of Establishing Long-Lasting Relationships 100

CHAPTER 4: LEGAL AND FINANCIAL MATTERS (UGH!) 103

The Boring Legal Stuff 104

Intellectual Property and Its Protection 107

Other Legal Protections 110

Raising Money for Your Business: Five Options 112

Taxes (More Ugh!) 115

CHAPTER 5: GROWING YOUR BUSINESS (IF THAT'S WHAT YOU WANT TO DO) 117

Assessing What You Want Your Business to Be and Do: Seven Things to Consider 118

Do You Need to Expand? Eight Signs that You Should . . . 121

How to Expand: Nine Ideas . . . 124

What about Licensing? Five Tips 128

Do You Need Employees? Seven Signs that You Do 131

Seven Ways to Locate the Right People 134

Nine Tips when Interviewing and Hiring 137

Legal and Financial Information about Employees 141

Ten Strategies for Keeping Your Business on Track for Growth . . 144

RESOURCES 148

Further Reading 149

Online Resources 151

About the Author 154

INDEX 155

ABOUT THE PUBLISHER 160

INTRODUCTION

This Book Will Teach You to Start Your Own Business is the perfect starting point for those who are considering jumping to another career track and going into business for themselves, whether they are fresh out of college or already in a traditional work environment. The thought is both exhilarating and scary! Entrepreneurship is praised as the ticket to greater things: work for yourself, set your own hours, do what you love with passion and creativity, and get rich! Unfortunately, these rosy descriptions tend to leave out a lot of the boring and hard day-to-day work that gets you there, things like taxes, legal issues, employees (if you need them), marketing, and dozens of other things. If you want to start your own business, how do you do it without falling into despair or just giving up?

This guide will teach you the basics and give you a good grounding for the foundations you'll need to lay in order to get started on the right footing. What goals are realistic? How much money can you invest? How much time can you invest? Should you keep your day job while planning out your new life in self-employment? (Yes, you should!) Brief but helpful discussions of all of these questions and much more will help you make the right choices and give your new business the chance it deserves to be the success you want it to be!

The book is divided into chapters arranged by subject matter. Each offers you important information and gives you places to start working from. It won't give advice for your specific industry, but instead offers information that you can apply in any work environment, with an emphasis on how to succeed by also giving back. This book is a handy reference and guide for when you need to check on something about a specific topic. You may already know some of this information, whereas other advice may be new to you. Read it in whatever order you wish, and feel free to dip into the text wherever it is helpful to you. Each chapter and each section can stand alone, but also holds together to give you the bigger picture.

A book of this size can only offer brief summaries of each subject, but take in this information and use it to launch into further research and education. The Resources section at the end gives you a lot of helpful further reading, as well as useful websites that can offer you far more information—especially concerning legal issues—than a small book can. Bear in mind that this book is not to be seen as a substitute for legal or any other kind of professional advice. Getting your career to where you want it to be doesn't have to be overwhelming and confusing. By using the tips and suggestions in this book, you can help further your own goals and get started on the path to the successful self-employed career that you want!

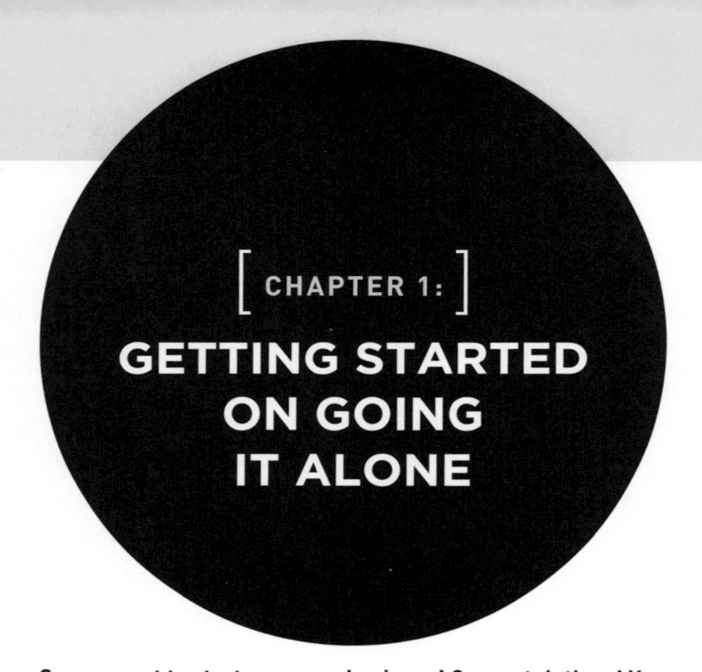

[CHAPTER 1:] GETTING STARTED ON GOING IT ALONE

So you want to start your own business! Congratulations! You are entering into a world that is exciting and terrifying in equal parts. Most people dream of working for themselves at some point, but actually making a commitment to go for it is a decision that far fewer ever take. There can be many reasons for this, some of which are beyond our control, such as personal and family commitments, job stability, and one's own physical and mental health. But if you're in the position to take a shot at being an entrepreneur, you're one of the lucky ones! Working for yourself is rewarding and potentially lucrative, but it can also be frustrating and demoralizing, so starting off with a realistic understanding of the process and possessing the right mindset are crucial to getting going. This chapter will give you some of the basics you need to get started on planning out your journey.

ELEVEN QUALITIES OF THE ENTREPRENEUR'S MINDSET

When starting out as a would-be entrepreneur, it's not enough to just have a dream or even a plan (though those are important, too!). To be able to successfully make a go of starting and running your own business, there are a number of important characteristics that you'll either need or have to cultivate. Here is a list of some of the things you should be striving for in yourself.

1. **The desire to make things happen:** Without this, you're going nowhere. You have to be committed to working for results and toward goals. If you don't want to do it, it just isn't going to happen, or at best, it will take a lot longer than it should. What do you really desire to do? You'll need to ask yourself that question, and keep asking yourself as you go along.

2. **The willingness to take action:** Having the desire to succeed is great, but then you have to be willing to do the work to implement your goals and strategies. It's not just about having initiative; you'll need to define where you must take action to implement your ideas and create realistic plans for doing so. And you'll have to revisit this constantly and always be observing where you could best take action next.

3. **The ability to think creatively:** If you're planning on starting your own business, you probably already do a fair amount of thinking outside of the box. If being in a standard workplace is not for you, examine ways in which you could do better for yourself. How do you think creatively in your personal life? What hobbies or interests do you have that require inventive thinking? What skills do you already have that you can bring to your proposed new business? Many entrepreneurs and coaches recommend writing morning pages, that is, jotting down your ideas and impressions when you wake up, before you've caffeinated or had the concerns of the day creep in. This is a great way to stimulate new ideas and see what comes bubbling up, and develop your creativity over time.

4. **The desire to be challenged:** Entrepreneurs love a challenge. If you're always looking for new ways to challenge and better yourself, you're already on the way. Do you love working on intellectual challenges or brainteasers? Do you throw yourself into a new project at your current job? Do you love rock climbing or other physical endurance tests? If so, you already have a valuable quality that you'll be able to bring into your new work.

5. **Being open to change:** Those who go it alone are almost always willing to accept that change is inevitable and is even something to welcome. If you need the sameness and security of a day job, then starting your own business isn't for you, because you'll be hit with new things (good and bad) almost every day. Being able to welcome that uncertainty will be essential.

6. **Feeling fear:** If you're unsure about all of this, that's a good sign! You shouldn't be cocky or get a false sense of security about your future. Being unsettled about what might happen if you don't succeed is a great way to keep you focused and committed. When you're no longer relying on a stable paycheck, you'll need to let that uncertainty fuel your drive.

7. **But also being fearless:** At the same time, fear can't hold you back. You'll need to understand what an acceptable risk is and how to manage it. You simply won't succeed without taking risks and making some leaps of faith. Confine your fear to worrying about what will happen if you *don't* make bold moves. This doesn't mean you should get reckless and risk your health, your safety, or your family's security, of course. It means that you understand the risks and commit to working through them.

8. **Never being satisfied:** Perfectionism has both good and bad points. At its best, you'll deliver an awesome project or task; at its worst, nothing ever gets done, because you never stop tinkering and won't let it go. This negative side is rooted in fear; you're actually afraid to let it go: Will it be criticized? Will people think it's not good enough? Never being satisfied means being able to let go of a thing that needs to go, and committing yourself to making the next one even better. It's not about it being good enough; it's about accepting that you did your best at this point, and that there's always room for improvement down the line.

9. **The willingness to listen and learn:** Even going it alone, you are not an island. In fact, you'll need others more than ever, because there are so many questions and topics about which you won't know enough that getting qualified advice is absolutely essential. Seek out absolutely everyone who can give you tips and insight. Read every book relevant to you that you can. The more you increase your knowledge and listen to others, the better your chances of success.

10. **Seeing other points of view:** In the process of seeking out others, you will invariably hear points of view and ideas that conflict with yours, in everything from basic philosophy to tips about the process.

This is a great thing, because it may give you ideas you hadn't thought about before. Even if you reject someone else's approach, be open to at least entertaining it as a possibility. There might be something in it that could work for you. We never know enough, and we can find wisdom in unlikely places if we look for it. Seek out and listen to people in industries completely different from yours, and see what you can find.

11. **The ability to learn from mistakes and failures:** Mistakes happen and you will fail; it's inevitable. Being able to roll with punches and come up standing will be crucial to your future success. You must be open to using each failure as a learning experience, to seeing what you can do to not to repeat it the next time. Try not to take these setbacks personally. Even the most seasoned of entrepreneurs still makes mistakes, gets a prediction wrong, or blows a potential opportunity. Use these frustrating times throughout your career as a way to move forward. Don't dwell on them or what might have been.

"The only thing worse than starting something and failing . . . is not starting something."

—SETH GODIN

WHAT KIND OF BUSINESS DO YOU WANT? NINE QUESTIONS TO ASK

This book cannot tell you what business or industry to go into; that will be entirely up to you. But before you begin with your plan, you have to know what it is you'll be doing. This may seem obvious, but it's remarkable how many people do go in with the idea that they will figure out the details as they go. Don't do this! Be very clear what kind of business you want, and what goods or services it will provide—right from the outset. You may need to tinker with this and change things as you go along, but the basic idea should not change too much. Here are some important questions to keep in mind.

1. **What do you most love doing?** Get a sheet of paper, and write down your interests and passions. Write down everything you can think of, from casual interests to the things you absolutely love. Read back through them. Which, if any, of these things might be a place where there could be a business need? Almost certainly you'll be able to identify a few ideas. If you have a passion for classic films, think about what you might be able to do that could service others with the same passion. Do you love gardening? There are endless numbers of options in that field. Take your time with this exercise; don't rush it. If you're trying to hone in on a

passion that could become a career, you need to devote a lot of time and thought to it.

2. **What do you not like?** Now make another list, this time writing down the things that you don't like. There are probably going to be many more items on this one! This is not just a list of gripes. Rather, it will give you some more options that can be paired with what you do enjoy. Is there a feature on your otherwise-great phone that really annoys you that an app could fix? If you love gardening, maybe you're annoyed that no one in your town has opened a quality nursery. Match the bad with the good and see if you can find problems within your passions that no one has yet solved. Find a need and fill it, as the old saying goes.

3. **What are you really good at?** Make yet another list, this time focusing on all of the things that you are great at doing. This can include your education and work skills (such as software, programming, and bookkeeping), but should also include soft skills (for example, phone skills and conflict management) and talents from your personal life. Do you play the violin? Do you make an amazing pasta primavera? Put it down. Do a brain dump of everything you think you're good at.

4. **At what places do these three lists cross?** Are there any areas where you can combine talents, irritations, and interests? These are likely candidates for the kind of self-employed work you should be looking at. Again, it might be good to sit with this for a while, as an obvious answer may not come up immediately. But you might find one or more areas where a viable business could be created.

5. **What is the target market for your idea(s)?** Once you've started zeroing in on some possible businesses and services, start

thinking about who might be the right target for what you want to offer. When looking at target markets, going smaller is almost always better. Never tell yourself, "Everyone will want this." No, they won't. Being realistic about who will buy your product or service is not only an exercise in humility; it will keep you grounded and better able to market and sell to the people that actually *do* want what you offer. A small market is not necessarily a bad thing. If you can attract a few thousand loyal customers, that's far better than marketing to millions of people who don't care.

6. **What need are you fulfilling?** You have ideas, you have one or more potential target markets, but what need will you be addressing? It's not enough to want to open a florist's shop, for example, or create a new dating app. What specifically about those things is needed by the market, by the community? What is it that you can offer as a florist that people want, but don't currently have? Dating apps are everywhere; what makes yours special and fixes some gripe that people have about the existing ones? Often, you don't have to offer something stunningly original; you just need to find a new angle on an old problem and offer it to people in a way that will make their lives easier.

7. **What are your competitors already doing?** If you have some idea about where you'd like to go with your self-employment, start looking at what your potential competitors are already doing in the field. And yes, you will probably have them, at least in some form. Even if you think of opening a shop in a small town that doesn't have another one selling something similar, people have other options: driving to a bigger town or shopping online. What are you going to need to do to convince potential customers that what you offer is better for them? How are you going to stand out? Research what similar businesses are doing so that you can get a sense of how it's done, but also ways that you might do it better.

8. **Are you being realistic?** Ask yourself this hard question. Is your proposed new business really going to fly? Obviously, you can't know for certain, and even small businesses that seemed promising for a year or two can be forced out of business by unforeseen circumstances. But given the limited amount that you do know, try to be realistic about whether or not your plan is viable. A small target market can be a good thing, but if it's too small, you won't be able to survive. A specialty shop that only attracts thirty customers is not going to survive, no matter how interesting and unique its wares are. Are there enough people out there to sustain your business in the long run?

9. **Are you willing to do the needed work?** Finally, if everything else is looking good so far, ask yourself more hard questions: Can you actually do this, and are you willing to put in the necessary work for it to really succeed? It's easy to be enthusiastic about a new project at the start of it, but as we all know, interest can fizzle once the novelty wears off. Is this something you're passionate enough about that it can survive the inevitable times of frustration and burnout? Can you keep going even when it looks like you're failing? Again, you may not be able to answer this until you're actually tested by it in real life, but look at your own work and personal history to see how you've risen to challenges in the past. This may be your best indication of how you'll handle future problems.

IDEAS VERSUS OPPORTUNITIES: THEY'RE NOT THE SAME THING!

At the start of your new business, you will be enthusiastic and maybe bursting with ideas, and that's great! The more you can bring to the table, the better. But understand that an idea and an opportunity are not necessarily the same thing. Something that you're sure will work just fine may slam into a proverbial brick wall in the real world. This section will help clarify the difference between the two. And you need both, incidentally.

- **Ideas:** Ideas are essential. They are the solutions to the problems you see and want to correct. Without them, you'll get nowhere. You need a constant stream of new ideas, and should always encourage creative thinking in yourself and others. But ideas on their own won't get you very far. They come at the very start of the process, but a good idea is not a guarantee of success, sorry to say. A good idea is always better than a bad idea (and sometimes you won't know which is which until you try them out!), but without the work to turn it into something more, it's just as useless to you.

- **Opportunities:** One definition of an opportunity is that it is an idea you can put into practice. Or it might not come from an idea, and instead be a circumstance that comes along at the right time, due to planning and strategy. Having a good idea is a fairly common occurrence (you'll

probably have them all the time), but a good opportunity is much rarer and deserves your attention. With hard work, an opportunity can lead to more business and has real value, whereas an idea only has the potential to be something if you follow up on it to turn it into an opportunity. It's often said that investors will not back your great idea, but they will back your great opportunity.

- **Turning an idea into an opportunity:** In order to turn your brilliant ideas into valuable opportunities, you'll need to take them through several steps.

- **Analyzing how your idea fits in:** What about your idea is needed right now? Is there a market for your idea, and how much of one is there? Can you actually fulfill that need or want in a viable and timely way, and, if so, what's the best way to go about doing it?

- **Creating a solid business plan:** You need to write down how you will plan out your idea. You'll have to go into some detail, so that you don't leave out any basic questions or potential big problems. The more you can identify at the start, the better understanding you'll get of your idea and if it will work. This can be painful, especially if it seems like your bright idea won't work after all, but it's a necessary part of the process.

- **Finding the right collaborators and information:** Whom will you need to help you along the way? Investors? Partners? Will you need legal advice? Tax advice? You may need some or all of these. What information will you need to collect and learn to help your idea along its path? Who will lead the process? Will it be you, or is there someone better suited to getting the whole thing off the ground?

- **Figuring out what else you'll need:** What other resources are going to be necessary to help your idea take flight and become a genuine opportunity? We mentioned investors above, so what will your budget be? The financial outlay will be a huge consideration as you move forward. Do you need a brick-and-mortar location, or can it all be done online, at least at first? Can you go it alone for a while, or will you need a team? Will there be employees? As you can see, getting an idea out of your head and into the real world can take a lot of work, but it's necessary!

> **"If you are working on a product that's going to be consumer-facing, then feedback is invaluable. You should be out there being brave and talking to people and asking for feedback as much as possible."**
>
> ***—EMILY BROOKE (COFOUNDER OF BLAZE)***

BRICK AND MORTAR VERSUS ONLINE: THE PROS AND CONS OF EACH

Depending on the nature of your business, it may need a physical location, or you may be able to start out entirely in the virtual world. The choice may be obvious in many cases, but it's not always as apparent as you might think. If you are selling specialty items, a shop might be ideal, but it's also possible to have a booming business in online-only orders. An app startup might be doable in your living room for a while, but it may grow to where you at least want some shared work space with your collaborators, where you can go and bounce ideas off each other. Both physical and virtual locations have their pros and cons; here are some considerations.

ONLINE PROS

- **It's far easier and cheaper at the outset:** It's obvious that simply starting with a website and a vision is far more financially easy and safe than worrying about renting office space, store space, and so on. You'll need to do some background work to get up and running, and, depending on the nature of the business, you'll need some capital investment, but it's far easier than also factoring the many issues involved with setting up a real-world location. For many, their businesses start online and transition to the real world later on.

- **It's more convenient:** Whatever the nature of your business, it's only a click away for you and your customers and clients. They can access it at any time of day or night. This is especially true for e-commerce; someone can order a product or service whenever they want to with the click of a button.

- **It potentially reaches far more people:** With the global reach of the internet, you can have visitors from literally all over the world at any time. Once you get known, your customer and client base can be truly international, giving you opportunities that weren't available to most businesses a generation ago. The potential for growth is almost unlimited.

- **It's more flexible:** Especially if it's a side business when you're starting out, you can work on it when you have the time, or in addition to your day job. You don't need to be on-site somewhere. Yes, you can sit on your couch and do the work you need on your business in the evenings after work. An online business can fit into and around your schedule.

- **It can be done anywhere.** If you're living above the Arctic Circle and want to start a coaching and consulting business, you can, thanks to the miracles of technology! Whatever you want to do is far less limited by geography than it used to be.

ONLINE CONS

- **Invisibility:** At the start, you are just one more page among millions. Who's going to notice? Who's going to care? You'll have to do a fair bit of shouting to get any attention, and there's nothing to differentiate you from a zillion other sites, at least at first. Your search engine optimization (SEO) has to be on point, and you'll still have to do a lot of real-world hustling for attention.

- **It's harder to build a reputation:** Going along with the invisibility issues, you'll struggle more to make a name for yourself at first. If you don't have a lot of face-to-face contact with clients and customers, it's going to be harder to win them over at the beginning. The personal connection still counts! You'll need some good social proof and word-of-mouth referrals to get people talking about what you do, and to make them care enough to go to your site.

PHYSICAL PROS

- **You can situate yourself in a good location:** Depending on the nature of your business and your budget, placing your business in a strategic location can pay off big. For stores, walk-in traffic can be huge if you're fortunate enough to have a location frequented by a lot of people every day.

- **The human contact element is there:** Whether it's a store that encourages browsing, or a software startup where people like to sit around tables and brainstorm, that direct human connection can be crucial to helping the business grow. If you and your partners don't meet regularly or only do so via online video chat, you may start to feel isolated and unproductive.

- **You have more presumed legitimacy:** A store is somehow more real if you can walk into it. A company presents itself as more professional if it has a physical address. It brings to mind the practice that some businesses still use of renting a post office box at a copy or mail center, and then referring to that number as a "suite" at the address of the business. To someone who doesn't know better, this looks very impressive!

- **There's still nothing quite like a store:** People still love shopping in stores. Being able to try out electronics or phones, being able to try on new clothes—there's a tactile, tangible element to it that gets lost in online retail, as convenient as it can be. Being able to take advantage of that and encourage customers to impulse buy or to cross-sell them something else is a great business opportunity. And you build the human connection and the chance of having repeat customers.

PHYSICAL CONS

- **The cost:** The fact is that physical locations are expensive, often very much so. Rent, bills, furnishings, insurance . . . it all adds up depressingly quickly. You'll be spending a whole lot more on a location than you will a website. You'll need to have a very good sense of your budget and what your finances will allow.

- **You're limited by location:** Your store or your office is where it is. That means that people need to come to you. If you can't afford to be in a busy downtown area, it's going to be harder to attract customers and clients. Not impossible, but it will take more willingness on their part to come to you, meaning you'll have to work harder on developing your brand and reputation.

- **You'll still need to be online:** You'll need to have an online presence. You'll need to be contactable outside of regular business hours, your shop may want to offer online sales to customers outside of your area, and your service may have additional information that customers need online. There's no escaping it: even with a real-world location, you're not going to be able to avoid being online, and you very likely don't want to anyway, as it's essential to any twenty-first century business. One of the few exceptions seems to be local restaurants, where an oddly high number of them don't seem to have much of an online presence at all. This may be partially because they *are* so locally focused, but even here, being able to have a site with information, menus, and a phone number seems crucial. Still, there you have it. If you're starting a restaurant, don't follow this model; have a well-designed and appealing website!

"The critical ingredient is getting off your butt and doing something. It's as simple as that. A lot of people have ideas, but there are few who decide to do something about them now. Not tomorrow. Not next week. But today. The true entrepreneur is a doer, not a dreamer."

—NOLAN BUSHNELL (FOUNDER OF ATARI)

A SOLE PROPRIETOR VERSUS A CORPORATION: WHICH IS RIGHT FOR YOU?

You'll need to consider how your business will be set up. In Canada, your basic formats are a sole proprietorship, a partnership, a corporation, and a cooperative. The United States also offers entrepreneurs the LLC (limited liability company), but these do not exist in Canada. Here is a description of each.

- **Sole proprietorship:** As the name implies, this is a business of one, namely you. It's unincorporated, which means that there is no legal separation between you and your business. You are responsible for any debts accrued, and if you are sued, you can be personally liable for damages. But fear not! The sole proprietorship is still the most popular format for small businesses for a number of reasons. It is by far the cheapest and easiest to set up, you don't need a board of directors, you make all of the decisions, and your taxes and accounting will be much simpler. You can always start out as a solo venture and incorporate later, if you need to.

- **Partnership:** This format is similar to a sole proprietorship; the main difference is that it consists of an agreement between two or more people to operate a business. In Canada, there are three types:

  - **General partnership:** This form of business is very similar to a solo business, with all partners being liable for debts and legal issues. It consists of an agreement between the parties on how the business will operate, and who will do what. This can be another cheap and easy way of getting a business going. Just be mindful that if someone else does something illegal, you can be personally liable for it. More on all of this in the next section.

- **Limited partnership:** A limited partnership is essentially a general partnership where one or more of the partners is given limited liability. These individuals may offer, for example, financial backing, but otherwise not be involved in the running to the business. A limited partnership may be seen as and set up as a corporation, so you'll have to determine if this is something you'll want to explore. A corporation is more likely to attract funding, if you need it.

- **Limited Liability Partnership (LLP):** An LLP gives the partners more protection, but these kinds of business ventures are usually only permitted for higher-risk professions, such as legal or medical. Each province has different laws regulating their formation and operation. You won't be able to create an LLP for your gourmet chocolate shop, sorry to say!

• **Corporation:** A corporation gives you full legal protection for your personal assets; if you are sued, you will not be personally liable for damages, only the company will. It is the most comprehensive form of business. It also is the one given the most respect, the type that attracts the most funding, and the one that you'll probably want to move into at some point in the future, if your business grows. The disadvantages are that corporations are more expensive to set up and have considerably more complex tax regulations. Also, you will need to decide if you want to incorporate federally or provincially.

- **Provincially:** This form can be far easier starting out, but it means that you are limited to conducting business in your own province.

- **Federally:** This form of incorporation allows you to conduct business across Canada, provided you register it in each province where you want to do business. You will also receive international recognition, and be able to use your name throughout the country. The disadvantages are (of course!) more paperwork, limits on the business name you can use (a name search will be conducted to prevent duplication), and the need to abide by both federal and provincial laws.

- **Cooperative:** This is another form of corporation. According to the Canadian government: "A co-operative is a legally incorporated corporation that is owned by an association of persons seeking to satisfy common needs such as access to products or services, sale of their products or services, or employment." A cooperative is owned by its members, who also use its services or products.

In general, the sole proprietorship is probably going to be your best bet at first. Give your business some time to stretch out and grow a little, before you see where you want to take it. For further information on how to establish any of these kinds of businesses, see the Online Resources portion of the Resources section.

GOING IT ALONE VERSUS HAVING PARTNERS

As mentioned in the previous section, you have the option of setting up your business on your own, or including others. Whichever choice you make will be determined by a number of factors: the type of business, your need for help, how well you work with others, and whether or not anyone is interested in your project. There are advantages and disadvantages to both, at least at the start. As your business grows, it's almost inevitable that you'll need to add other people, whether as partners or employees, to keep things running. Here is a look at some of the benefits and drawbacks of having partners when you're first starting out.

BENEFITS OF HAVING PARTNERS

- **You have more than one person with expertise and skills.** Obviously, it's going to be difficult for you to do everything, so having someone with, say, web design skills, while someone else is a whiz with accounting and taxes is going to make your life a lot easier. Maybe you're not so good with marketing, but your friend is. Having two or more people working toward a common goal, each bringing their own specialties, is a great way to move the process along much faster.

- **There's a shared financial input.** If you are all equally committed to the business, then each person will probably be expected to invest a certain amount of their money and time. This may be an equal amount for each person, or it may be divided up in other ways, as you see fit. Doing this takes some of the burden off each of you, and lets you get on with putting the business together without having to worry about running out of money, at least not right away. The more partners you have, the less your initial outlay will probably have to be.

- **There's shared risk.** Tied in with investment, it also means that if the business suffers a loss, it will be less for each person involved, since the money is pooled. And it's entirely possible that your business will lose money for a while before seeing a profit. It's better when it's not all your money, all the time.

- **You have the chance for better networking.** You're not going to know everyone you need to know, but bringing in a partner or two will potentially double or triple (or more) your network. Your partner may know a great business lawyer or tax accountant that will save you time and money. Another partner may have access to some great marketing people, or an ad agency that gives discounts. Always consider the possibility of friends of friends, and how much that can help you in the early days.

- **You'll get support and friendship.** You'll have great days and not-so-great days. With partners, you can share in the job together and pat each other on the backs, but you also can commiserate when things go wrong, or get a pep talk when you need it. Don't discount the importance of a mutual support network. It can keep you going when things get tough, and spur you to greater things after an initial success or two.

DRAWBACKS OF HAVING PARTNERS

- **There is a potential for greater personal risk.** Since every partner shares in the liabilities, you will all be responsible for any losses or mistakes made. If one of the partners makes a bad business decision, even innocently, it could come back to haunt you all. If a partner does something foolish or illegal, you all are in potential trouble over it. Unfortunately, the only way you can prevent this is to go solo, or to be absolutely sure that you trust those you're partnering with.

- **You have to go along with the group.** You won't have complete autonomy anymore. If this project is your baby and you feel particularly protective about it, you need to consider whether you'll be able to share it with anyone else, at least for a while. Because once partners are in the mix, they will have a say, and it may not always be the one you'll like. You'll have to be willing to compromise and meet your partner(s) halfway, or things will get difficult very quickly.

- **You need to define roles and rankings very clearly.** Is everyone equal, or are there divisions of authority? Technically, a "partnership" is just that, but maybe one of your partners doesn't want the same level of responsibility. Also, be very clear on who is doing what. In some cases, it will be necessary for partners to wear many hats, and their jobs may cross over, but try to define each person's role as clearly as you can from the outset, making allowances for the fact that conditions change.

- **What if one partner turns out to be difficult?** You may think you know your friend(s) and that they would be excellent to work with, but what if that turns out not to be the case? Aside from any legal or financial worries, what if the person is just a pain to work with? You'll have to think carefully about the kind of partnership agreement that you sign. Do you have any way of voting out a partner if the others agree? What if you're only partnered with one other person? How do you dissolve the partnership and still keep the business as yours? These are hard questions that have no definite answers. Again, be very sure whom you're partnering with.

- **It may test your friendship.** If you start out a new business with your friends, be aware that difficulties could come up that will cause friction and fracture. Sometimes, friends are better left as friends, and not business partners. Be very sure that the individuals you decide to partner with are either good enough friends that you can face the bad times together, or faraway enough acquaintances that if you never saw them again after the partnership dissolved, it wouldn't matter too much to you.

- **What if someone wants out?** Following on from the previous entry, what if a partner wants to leave? Do they have a legal means of doing so? This is something to consider, because people leave businesses and companies all the time, and not only over antagonistic reasons. The person might be moving away, or might have been offered a new job that they really want to take. What do you do then? What if you decide you want to leave your own business behind and let someone else have it? You need to have an exit strategy to prevent any hassles later on, preferably worked into your initial agreement.

CRAFTING AN EXCELLENT BUSINESS PLAN: NINE ESSENTIAL COMPONENTS

Now that you have some ideas about the nature of your business and its composition, it's time to start thinking about a business plan. A good, solid business plan is absolutely essential to whatever you have in mind, and while it won't guarantee you success, without it you pretty much have no chance. You'll absolutely need a well-written business plan to attract investors and financiers, and maybe even partners, if you're looking outside your immediate social circle (and even your friends will probably want to see it, too!). A well-crafted business plan can be a great thing to show any potential employees, if you're looking to hire someone early on. Even if you're just creating it for yourself, it's an important document that will give you guidance, and to which you can return when you need to make changes and adjustments. Here are the basic elements of a solid business plan.

1. **Executive summary:** As the name implies, this is a summary of your business: what it is, what it does, the mission statement, what the products or services are, who the key players in the company are (including yourself), the location (if there is one), and all other pertinent information. You should keep it short: no more

than two pages. Think of it as a written elevator pitch. If you are looking for funding, you should include some financial information here and direct them to the appendix for more details (see below). It may actually be a good idea to leave writing it until last, after you're clear about everything and can summarize it better.

2. **Company description:** In this section, go into detail about what your business is and what needs it addresses or problems it solves, whether for customers, clients, the general public, or other businesses. Identify the key players on your team, even if you are the only one at the moment. What expertise do you and any partners bring with you? How will this give you an edge over your probable competition? If you are planning on opening a physical location, where will it be and why?

3. **What you offer in terms of products or services:** Go into detail about what you plan to offer. What is unique about your product or service, how will it address specific needs, and what will make it better than other comparable offerings from other companies? Does anything you plan require legal hurdles, such as patents or other licensing? Put it in here. You need to get into some detail, both for your own clarity and for that of anyone who might be providing funding or considering partnering with you. You have to be able to convince them that what you offer is viable and can make money.

4. **Market analysis and opportunities:** This will be your research on your potential target market(s), as well as on the industry itself. Who is interested in what you offer? The more detailed and focused you can make your markets, the better. No one wants to hear that your product is for "everyone." It's not. Who are your competitors? What is the industry like at the moment? Is it growing, staying the same, or contracting? What do the longer-term projections look like? Where will your business fit in?

5. **Management and organization summary:** How will your business be set up? Will it be a sole proprietorship, a partnership, or a corporation? What legal papers will you need to file and have on hand? How will the company itself be structured? If there are partners, is there a CEO, a COO, VPs, etc.? If you have partners, make sure to include their resumes and CVs as well; you want to show that each of you is qualified and able to do the job they are being tasked with.

6. **Marketing and sales strategy:** You'll need to devise a basic strategy. This will invariably change over time as you learn what works and what doesn't, but you need to have something down that gives you a starting point for how you will market and sell. For more on these topics, see chapter 3.

7. **Funding needs:** How will your business be financed? Do you have enough money to do it yourself at the outset? Or will you need some kind of funding? This might be in the form of a business loan (debt), venture capital and financing (equity), etc. Use this section to outline what your projected costs will be over the first month, six months, year, and five years, and how you will need to meet those costs. Also, describe the terms you would like and/or need for any funding that you do receive.

8. **Financial outlook and forecast:** This will be more difficult if you are just starting out, but try to give some sense of what the financial outlook will be in your future. You're trying to show how the business will be stable and will grow over time, so don't go wild with crazy predictions of massive success. Slow and steady growth projections will be more convincing. You may feel like you're just grasping around in the dark for these numbers, but if you can work out details including sales projections,

a profit-and-loss statement, a balance sheet, and so on, you'll have a better sense of what you are aiming for.

9. **Appendix:** Many business gurus recommend that you include a section at the end for additional documents that are relevant to your plan. This can include everything from credit reports and resumes/CVs to legal documents, patents, and recommendations and testimonials. Investors and legal advisers will want to see as much supporting documentation as you can provide, so be prepared to go overboard on this section!

Whew! And you just wanted to start a simple small business! The thing is, it's not all that simple, and if you're really serious about growing your small business into something bigger, you have to make the effort to get this information together right at the start, for your own sake as much as anyone else's. You may not want to let your new business blossom into a giant corporation; you may be quite content to use it as a side business for extra income, or only need it to grow far enough to meet your own needs. This is entirely fine, but having this information at hand will still benefit you greatly, so make the effort to get together as much of it as you can. Take your time and learn about each of these steps, so you can do them right. You'll learn a lot in the process, and save yourself time and trouble later on.

EIGHT TIPS FOR SETTING AND MEETING YOUR GOALS

It should go without saying that in order to run a small business and make it successful, you have to get good at setting goals and working to achieve them. It's essential to have road signs along the way, so you know where you are, where you've come from, and where you're going. Your goals will be both short term and long term, and you'll need to have plenty of both. It will be crucial that you commit to working toward them and doing everything you need to do according to the schedule that you lay out for yourself. And this is the trick: there may be no one else to keep you on track. So you'll have to learn to be self-disciplined. If this idea seems difficult or impossible, here are some ways to set goals and keep yourself on track.

1. **Understand your goals.** This seems obvious, but you have to know what each goal is and why you have it. What purpose is it serving in the larger picture? Even if it's a small, immediate thing that you need to do by the end of the week, ask yourself why. How will that help you along? How does it fit into the bigger picture? Every goal and aim should be working toward something. Also, be mindful of what will happen if you don't meet this goal on time. It may be relatively minor, such as you'll just have to work on it over the weekend, but it could

be critical, like a deadline for a funding application. Always be aware of the consequences of letting goals go.

2. **Be specific about each goal.** You need to be as detailed as you can with each goal that you set. Just saying that you'd like to open a bakery next year will obviously not cut it! Take the time to define your goals and go into detail about how you might achieve them. Even if you're not sure how to go about it, write down the things you think you'll need to do. Do this for both long-term and short-term goals. Start with short-term goals, since these will be easier to define and easier to create a plan to achieve; it's less work to plan out how to get something done by the end of the month than by the end of the year. It may be something as simple as reading a book on entrepreneurship over the next two weeks. Practice on the smaller goals and work your way up!

3. **Break tasks down into smaller components.** Looking at one huge goal will likely be intimidating and demoralizing. You need to break down these bigger goals into smaller chunks that can be done more easily and across time. Everything adds up to the bigger goal that way, and you won't feel so overwhelmed. Set yourself time frames for working on smaller pieces of the goal and watch it get closer over time. Be patient.

4. **Always be realistic about what you can do.** You may start off ready to launch yourself into a huge project, only to find that the wind goes out of your sails a week or two later. Be careful and pace yourself, and don't bite off more than you can chew. Ask yourself what you can realistically accomplish in a given time frame. This may be affected by outside factors, such as your day job, family commitments, and more. You may not have sufficient knowledge or the skills to take care of some things on your list. It's very important to know what you don't know and to

ask for help when you need it. If you're unsure, get clear before starting into something only to find that you can't finish it. That's frustrating and a waste of your time.

5. **Make a schedule and keep to it!** Doing things when you feel like it or get around to them will lead you nowhere fast. If you have goals, you need to create a schedule and stick to it. If you have problems doing this, get a friend or family member to politely (or not so much!) nudge you to keep at it. Again, breaking your bigger tasks down into smaller ones will make it for easier for you to stick to your own schedule and not feel like you're overwhelmed. Look for ways that you can work on bigger tasks on a daily basis, so that a little gets done each day. Before long, you'll see how well you're progressing. Again, make sure that you or someone you trust is gently kicking your behind to keep you at it! Being accountable to someone is a great way to keep you on track.

6. **Measure your achievements.** Check off things as you complete them. Not only does this help you keep track of where you are, but it's also a little morale boost when you feel like you're not getting anywhere, or not moving fast enough. These kinds of small wins can help you stay focused on the bigger prize. Reward yourself once in a while with something chocolate or a gourmet coffee as a way of thanking yourself for a job well done, but don't let it go to your head; you still have a lot to do!

7. **Be ready for the unknown.** Without exception, things will go wrong. You'll get sidetracked, something at your day job will come up and take your time away, a family or friend issue will arise, the weekend you'd set aside to work only on your new business will slip away. You can't prevent these kinds of things from happening, so just accept that sometimes you'll have to take a detour. None of these distractions are necessarily big problems, and if you go in expecting that they'll happen

from time to time, you won't get caught out. Try to build a little time into your schedule in anticipation of these problems, and if they don't happen, then you'll be ahead. Don't take them personally, and don't get discouraged. Your goals need to be flexible and malleable to a certain extent anyway, and maybe a temporary setback will lead you to think of something you hadn't thought of before. Always be looking for a learning opportunity.

8. **Always monitor your own progress.** As with measuring your achievements, it's essential to keep track of where you are on the path to goal attainment. This is a form of built-in accountability, when you don't have a friend breathing down your neck to get something done! Check in with yourself regularly, maybe once a week for shorter-term goals and once a month for the longer-term ones, or whatever suits you and your schedule. But make sure you do it! Keeping track of where you are and what you need to do next will also prevent you from letting things slide until next week or next month, etc., which can be very easy to do when you're feeling overwhelmed or distracted. Monitoring your progress should become a habit that you get into, and the more you do it, the easier it will get.

STAY AT YOUR JOB, OR QUIT AND BOLDLY FORGE AHEAD ON YOUR OWN? (HINT: STAY AT YOUR JOB)

It should be no secret that if you are about to launch into a new business of your own, you still need stability and personal safety. Therefore, it's crucial to emphasize that when deciding to make a go of things on your own, *do not quit your day job*! It may seem like it will be difficult to do both; how can you invest the time you need when you're at an office from 9 to 5 every day? And yes, this *can* be a real problem. What it most likely means is that you won't be able to get your business off the ground as quickly as you'd like, and you'll need to wait a bit longer and be patient. But that's not a bad thing. You don't want to rush the process. Here are some tips for balancing the two and keeping things in perspective.

- **You can use the time to transition:** If you've mainly worked standard hours for a boss, you may not know how well you'll handle being on your own and making all the decisions. It might all seem like it will be fine, but you could discover that you're not as good at some aspects of self-employment as you thought you were. Being your own boss is a lot harder than it looks. Keeping the day job will allow you to experiment with wearing different self-employed "hats," while still being able to stick to the schedule you're familiar with for the time being. As you get more comfortable with the new roles and duties you'll be taking on, you'll have a better sense of how you'll do when you finally take away the safety net of the day job.

- **It keeps your income incoming:** The most important thing about not quitting is that you'll need a steady income while you're feeling things out and figuring out what will work and what won't. The security of that is worth far more than the free time you think you'll have by just jumping into the unknown. Start setting aside some of your income into savings so that you will have money saved up when the time comes to step out onto your own. This means that you'll probably have to ease off on social activities and expensive outings like drinks and dinners, but if you're committed to making the new business a reality, you need to be willing to sacrifice some indulgences now for the greater good later.

- **You can use the motivation:** Going it alone can be, well, lonely. You may find yourself spending a lot of hours planning, brainstorming, and working out details for your new business, to the exclusion of your friends and other social activities. If nothing else, hanging on to your day job allows you to keep tabs with others. Also, maybe something you're working on at your job can give you insights into how to solve a problem with your potential new business. Don't close the doors too soon, because you may have resources that can help you, as long as you're not violating company policies. Even if you hate your job and can't wait to quit, stick with it for a while longer. Use your dislike of it to spur you on to make your own business a reality. The longer you can tough it out, the better you'll feel when you actually can leave.

- **You might be able to work out a deal:** If your business is starting to take off and you need to devote more time to helping it along, you may be able to stick with your day job for a while, if it's mutually beneficial to you and your employer. Maybe you can work from home for a day or two per week, or work ten fewer hours a week. If your company is going through any kind of trouble, it might be a welcome offer. On the other hand, if they say no, you'll have to decide what works best. It's never easy making the leap, even when your business is showing promise.

- **It keeps you from feeling overwhelmed:** By necessity, you won't be able to work as long on your personal project each day, which means it will take longer to get going. This can actually be a benefit, because, while you may get impatient, it will also keep you from jumping in too deeply all at once and trying to do too much work. You'll be forced to pace yourself based on the hours that you actually have, and won't take on too much too fast. Nothing kills your enthusiasm and motivation like burning out too fast! Let your day job put the brakes on your new business, at least a little, and use the time you have to better effect.

- **You can keep it to yourself and experiment:** By working at your new business on the side, you can keep quiet about it until you're ready to tell the world. This is helpful if it's a great new and innovative idea that you don't want out in the world before it's ready. It also allows you time to try different approaches to see what works best, not only in the business itself, but also in your life as you make the transition into self-employment. It's best not to say too much to too many people at the start, anyway, and keeping your day job is a great cover for your bigger plans!

- **You won't feel rushed:** Knowing you have a steady job means that you can take all the time you need to get your new business off the ground. It pays to take the time to do it right. If you rush things, you may miss important details, make mistakes, and regret it sooner rather than later. Working really well on something a little at a time will produce a better product in the long run, so that when you're ready to launch your new business for real, everything will have been worked out. If it's valuable to you, it's worth taking the time to do it right. Holding on to your regular source of income is the best way to ensure that you won't feel pressured to rush things.

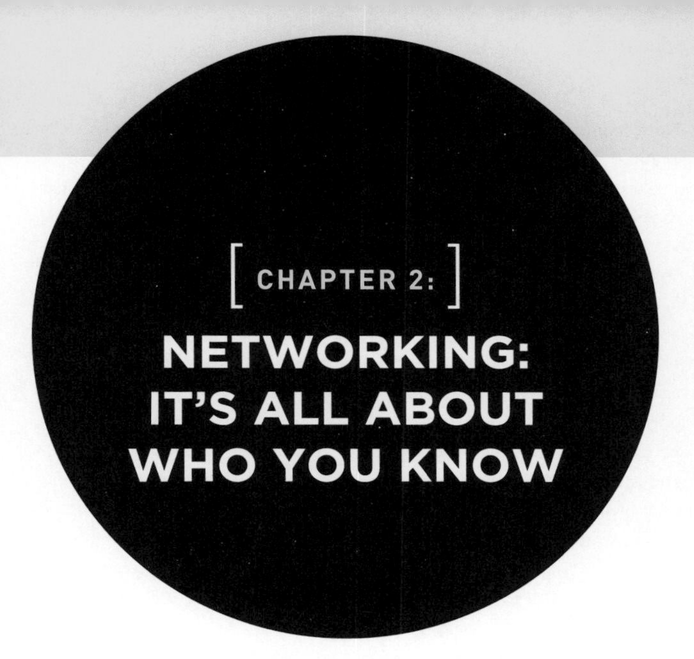

[CHAPTER 2:]

NETWORKING: IT'S ALL ABOUT WHO YOU KNOW

To get your business off the ground, and keep on growing it, networking is absolutely, completely essential, whether you want to or not. That's the not-so-great news. The better news is that networking is far easier today than ever before, and whether you're the most out-there extrovert or a stay-at-home introvert, there are ways to network that you can use, and feel comfortable doing. For introverts, some of the best networking around can be done in a one-on-one conversation over lunch or coffee. For extroverts, there are no shortage of conferences and events that you can dive into. And the good thing about networking is that it tends to get easier the more you do it, just like any other skill. So even if you're new to all of it, you can become a champion networker in time!

Networking, as the name implies, expands the circle of whom you know, and whom those people know. It's often with those friends of friends that you'll make some really valuable connections, the ones that can bring great benefits to you in the longer term. Networking keeps you up on what's happening in your industry, alerts you to upcoming problems, helps you keep an eye on competitors, and much more.

There is no single way to network, which is great, because you can pick and choose what you want to do. But networking can be done wrongly, and you can waste time and not get results. One of the most important things to remember is that you should never go in to a networking situation focused only on what you can get out of it. Yes, you want to meet people that can be of help to you, now and in the future, but you should also be thinking about what you can bring to the table to help others. What problems can you solve? What value might others see in you? The more you approach new contacts with this mindset, the more you will forge genuine connections not based on "What's in it for me?" And it's precisely these genuine connections that will serve you over time, since you'll have real friends and colleagues, and both sides will be doing good.

"The fastest way to change yourself is to hang out with people who are already the way you want to be."

—REID HOFFMAN (COFOUNDER OF LINKEDIN)

FIVE WAYS OF CULTIVATING NEW RELATIONSHIPS

As mentioned in the chapter introduction, the way to cultivate contacts is through an approach of giving rather than just receiving. You should meet each new contact with the idea of bringing something of value to them. Listen to them, hear their story, and see if there are ways that you can assist them in a meaningful way. Building relationships based on this kind of trust is a great feeling and establishes you as someone in your industry that others can admire and rely on. And having a good reputation is worth its proverbial weight in gold, far more than making a quick sale or getting a one-time favor. Here are some things to think about as you begin to reach out to others.

1. **Make the effort to connect.** This is the starting point. Nothing is going to happen until you commit yourself to contacting the people you want to contact. It's easy to sit around thinking about it, but you have to take action. That may seem scary, and you may be racked with doubt and feelings of self-consciousness, but honestly you're no different than anyone else starting out. Every great business started with ideas, and great business leaders were once nobodies. So take the time to start identifying people in your industry that you would like to reach out to. It doesn't just have to be CEOs, celebrities, and the like (though there's nothing wrong with having such people on your list!). Who are the everyday people doing great work? Maybe another shop owner on the other side of town? Maybe a charity that you admire? An awesome web

designer whom you might like to work with? The possibilities are endless! Start making lists of potential people to meet, divided up however seems right to you. Start small with peers, and save the bigwigs for a little later, if that feels safer to you.

2. **Have a genuine conversation.** When talking with a new connection, make sure that you're not talking at them. Give them plenty of time to talk about themselves and their work. Many studies have shown that just listening to someone else is a great way to build empathy and trust. Be the person who cares, the one whom they can trust. Value their story and mean it.

3. **Be willing to help.** As you listen, try to find out if they are wrestling with any problems of their own. You may not know the answer, but it will help you assess your own situation and any issues you may have to deal with eventually. But who knows? Maybe you do have some advice for them, or know someone who does. If you can help or put them in touch with someone who can fix things, you've built a strong connection that will likely stand up over time. And, when you need help at some point, they might be able to assist you.

4. **Connect them with others.** Even if you don't know anyone who can immediately help them with their concerns, it's great to introduce them to people you think they should know. They'll probably be more than happy to return the favor at some point. And it might not be just about other people. If you know of an event, conference, online group, an app or software, or even a periodical, blog, or newsletter that would help them, share the information. It's all about spreading the information wealth around. You can lift each other up.

5. **Make sure that you value the contact.** Anyone who is taking time out to talk to you, to share ideas, brainstorm, or even just to chat is someone that has great value. They don't need to take the time to talk to you, but obviously they see the value in you by doing so. Make sure that you reciprocate. If you don't value the other person and just try to use them or be deceitful in any way, word of it will get around, and there's not much you can do to get a good reputation after that happens! Be ethical, be kind, and look to serve others as best as you can.

> **"So often people are working hard at the wrong thing. Working on the right thing is probably more important than working hard."**
>
> ***—CATERINA FAKE (COFOUNDER OF FLICKR)***

YOUR NETWORK AT YOUR JOB: FIVE ACTIONS TO TAKE

If you are still working your day job while getting your new business off the ground (and you should be; see page 40 in chapter 1), you may be tempted to reach out to colleagues. This might be OK, but be very careful about what you say. It's one thing to have a side job to bring in some extra money, but if you intend to eventually make this your full-time job, you need to be careful about what you say and to whom. Unless everyone, including your boss, knows that you'll be leaving in the not-too-distant future, it could get very awkward if word gets around that you're planning on bailing. With that being said, there are some ways that you can use your professional network to your advantage while you're waiting to take the plunge into working for yourself.

1. **Keep tabs on those at your company that might be worth knowing.** It never hurts to reach out to people and make connections, especially beyond just your department. These could be individuals in other departments, other offices, maybe other branch locations that are a part of the same company. These are people who will probably be less invested in whether or not you remain with the company, but who might be good to know going forward. This is especially true if you are seeking out any individuals whose work is related to what you'll be doing on your own.

2. **Make sure they know how to get in touch.** This is obvious, but you'll need to be contactable, and not just at your work contacts. If you have a work email or a company Slack account, that's all well and good for the moment, but if you leave, how will they get in touch? Of course, you can just email them, but you might want to inform them of your website, your email list, your LinkedIn profile, and other methods of contacting you. Whether or not you want to give out a personal phone number or other such information is up to you; each situation will be different.

3. **Be ready in case they do want to meet.** Whether it's while you're still at your job, or sometime after you leave, always be prepared to meet up with someone at their convenience. If you've cultivated a relationship with a work colleague, they may be able to help you out on a problem you're struggling with. Conversely, wouldn't it be amusing if your new business involves servicing clients just like your former company, who, it turns out, needs what you do?

4. **Cultivate relationships with professional people elsewhere.** While you're working at your job, there's nothing to prevent you from using the professional tools at your disposal to reach out to others at different companies; you may as well get started on the networking thing as soon as possible. But again beware of how much you say and to whom. Also be aware of not abusing your professional privileges. You cannot share any privileged company information (nor use it for your own benefit), and you shouldn't be spending a lot of time networking on your company's time. But certainly, making connections while at your current job with your title and responsibilities will provide social proof in the future that you can do what you say you do.

5. **Leave on good terms.** If at all possible, try to leave your job with a handshake, a smile, and a farewell. Maybe you'll even get a little good-bye party out of it? That way, you will feel more comfortable reaching out to your former boss and colleagues in the future. They might be interested in what you're up to, and offer their assistance.

> **"Ignore the hype of the startups that you see in the press. Mostly, it's a pack of lies. Half of these startups will be dead in a year. So, focus on building your business so you can be the one left standing."**
>
> ***—JULES PIERI (COFOUNDER AND CEO OF THE GROMMET)***

PROFESSIONAL NETWORKS

There are different kinds of professional networks out there, beyond just reaching out to people one-on-one. While this should always be a central focus of your networking, here are a few other ways that you can connect with like-minded professionals.

- **Casual networks:** These kinds of networks are, just like they sound, informal in nature. They can be simple meetups for people in the same industry, a talk given by someone on a topic relevant to people working in that industry, or just social mixers for people who want to meet to have a chance to chat and make connections. Chambers of commerce, libraries, career associations, and more might sponsor these kinds of meetings, and it's worth having a look at your local business listings to see if anything like this is coming up that would appeal to you.

- **Contact networks:** A contact network is something of a holy grail for an independent businessperson. They are groups of specialists, usually one each in a collection of related businesses that rely on each other for referrals and word-of-mouth marketing. Think of a series of housing contractors. This kind of network might have an electrician, a plumber, a general contractor, a gardener, a roofer, a household appliance vendor, a landscaper, a window designer, and so on. Then, as each works on houses for various clients, if they discover that this same client needs one of these other services, they can be right there with the other contractor's business card or contact details. The word-of-mouth referral is a fantastic way of getting your name in front of others; all you have to do is

reciprocate. Everyone advertises everyone else, and in theory, everybody benefits. If you can get yourself into one of these kinds of networks, do it!

- **Professional associations:** These associations are devoted to a single industry or specialty profession. They generally don't hold public gatherings and may require membership to take part (which can be expensive). They may sometimes require certain conditions, such as professional credentials, to become a member. You may have to have been in business for a certain amount of time, or have had a certain number of clients, a certain amount of annual revenue, or other qualifications. Sometimes such groups allow associate members, so it might be worth your time to look into any that interest you. If you can get in with such an association, it will give you "street cred," and may open a number of doors for you in the future.

YOUR NETWORK IN YOUR PERSONAL LIFE: NURTURING RELATIONSHIPS WITH THOSE YOU ALREADY KNOW

One of the best places to start your networking journey is with those already closest to you: friends and family. These are the people who know you and (presumably!) like you the best, and who are likely to be your biggest fans at the outset of your self-employment journey. Don't hesitate to talk to them about your plans, your concerns, your dreams for world domination, and anything else that comes up. There might be some surprising help available to you from your closest sources.

- **Friends:** Depending on how many friends you have and what they do, you might have a wealth of contacts and information already available for you just by asking. Who among them is working in the really interesting jobs or industries that might be good for you to get in with? Ask around and see who's doing what; let them know what you're up to, and you'll probably find that there's some real interest and more than a few interesting contacts to be made.

- **Family:** Seriously, who else wants you succeed as much? Think about not just your immediate family, but also those who are a little more distant, and see who might have some ideas for you. Maybe you have a cousin working for a great company that could be a potential client. Does your uncle know someone who's great at marketing? Has your aunt built up a great list of contacts over the years? These can all be easy ways to introduce you to new and valuable people.

- **College contacts:** Whether you're just out of college or attended back in the Dark Ages, you undoubtedly made some great connections. Not just friends, but professors, advisers, and others who were invested in seeing you succeed. Imagine how they might feel if you reached out now to let them know what you're up to? Is there anything in your new work that may be of use to them? Reconnect in the spirit of giving and see where it takes you.

- **Former bosses and coworkers:** You note the emphasis here on "former." If you've worked various jobs in the past, and you've left those on good terms, consider reaching out to one or more of your former colleagues and even managers to let them know what you're up to. Take someone out to lunch or coffee and catch up. Is your previous employer one that might benefit from the services your new business provides? Slip that into the conversation!

- **Charities and community services:** One of the best ways to enter networking in the spirit of giving is to look to local charities and nonprofits. What are you doing that is aligned with what they are doing, and what can you offer them in the spirit of donation and volunteering? What charities and organizations align with your values that you would love to give something back to? Can you help a certain charity with an ongoing issue, something related to your new business? There might be a whole market for gearing some of your work toward the nonprofit industry. Don't worry about what they can do for you; give first, and let doors open naturally. And even if they don't, you've still added value to the world and done the right thing. That plus a genuine connection, and maybe a good reputation, are sometimes all you need.

> **"[Don't] let anyone convince you that your dream, your vision to be an entrepreneur, is something that you shouldn't do. What often happens is that people who are well meaning, who really care for us, are afraid for us and talk us out of it."**
>
> ***—CATHY HUGHES***

NETWORKING ONLINE WITH SOCIAL MEDIA

Today, it's easier than ever to reach out to people, anywhere in the world. That's both a blessing and a curse, but it can be one of your greatest assets. Whether you like social media or loathe it, it's not going anywhere, and you simply must take advantage of it when growing your network. Just about everyone is on one social media site or another, and it pays for you to be, too. You may have genuine concerns, but a business page is different from a personal page, and you want to keep it detached and more professional, anyway. Depending on the nature of your business, some social media platforms may be more beneficial to you than others.

LINKEDIN

LinkedIn is the premier social media site for business. It's the one place you need to be, no matter what industry you're in and what services or products your business intends to offer. It's essential that you keep your LinkedIn profile up-to-date and filled out with all relevant information. Consider it your online resume and a virtual brochure for your business. When updating, turn off your notifications; your contacts don't need to be bothered with that information. And when searching out new potential contacts, you may wish to do so anonymously. Don't just use the generic "join my network" option. Make the effort to reach out to people personally and build a connection, such as in a group (see below). Your connections will be much more valid. People are not trading cards, and you don't need to collect them all. Build connections that are meaningful, personal, and relevant.

NEWSGROUPS

LinkedIn has its own groups devoted to every business topic you can imagine, and it's well worth your time to take a wander into a few of them and introduce yourself. Be careful that you don't go in trying to promote yourself and sell things, however, or you'll be ignored quickly and maybe even kicked out. Go in with the spirit of discussing topics that interest you, meeting new people, and offering your help to those who might need it. Get known and get to know other users, and connect with them. Once you've been there a little while, you can open up a bit about what you're doing, but you never want to come off as selling something. There are many other newsgroups out there, of course, and you should investigate different platforms to see what's devoted to the topics that are relevant to you. Approach them with the same professionalism and respect.

OTHER SITES AND SOCIAL MEDIA

You may find that some other social media sites are useful to you as well, such as Twitter, Instagram, and the always controversial Facebook. Many businesses do use these sites successfully, and it's worth considering doing the same. If you do use Facebook and Twitter, here are some important points to remember:

- **Dos:** Keep your page professional, and always use images that are appropriate to your business. If you have a logo and other related designs, make sure you feature them. You want people identifying your page with your brand. Make sure that your about page or basic information is filled out and up-to-date. Put all relevant contact information where it can be easily found. Respond to all messages as promptly as you can (unless they're

spam, of course!). Post content regularly, at least once a day (and preferably more with Twitter). Post things that are relevant to your business, but also can be of interest to those who will see them: links to articles, videos, tutorials, and more—anything that you find interesting and helpful can be a great way to keep yourself in your followers' minds. Of course it's fine to let them know about your great new product or service, especially in the run-up to its release. But don't make that your only message. See below.

- **Don'ts:** Make your page all about you. Yes, that may seem strange, but you don't want to be proclaiming how great you are or what your latest product is with everything you post. You want to give your followers value. You are there to engage with them, not try to sell to them every day. If they are interested in what you offer, they'll seek you out. Also, don't post random things, just because you feel like you must post *something*. If there really isn't anything of value, let it go for the day. Be careful about posting too much humorous or political content, unless your business is related to those topics.

- **General advice:** When posting anything, always make a comment about what it is and why you're sharing it; give your followers some context. Use hashtags on Twitter to widen the potential for your post being seen. Make sure your link URLs are short (a necessary thing on Twitter). Just as importantly, keep your commentary relatively short. You don't need to include a whole essay in your post, just a few sentences about what you're sharing and why it's important. Make sure your posts are well-written and edited properly for grammar and spelling (especially with Twitter, which doesn't allow editing). You need to present professionally at all times. Ask your followers interesting questions and get them to actually engage with you, not just read what you're posting.

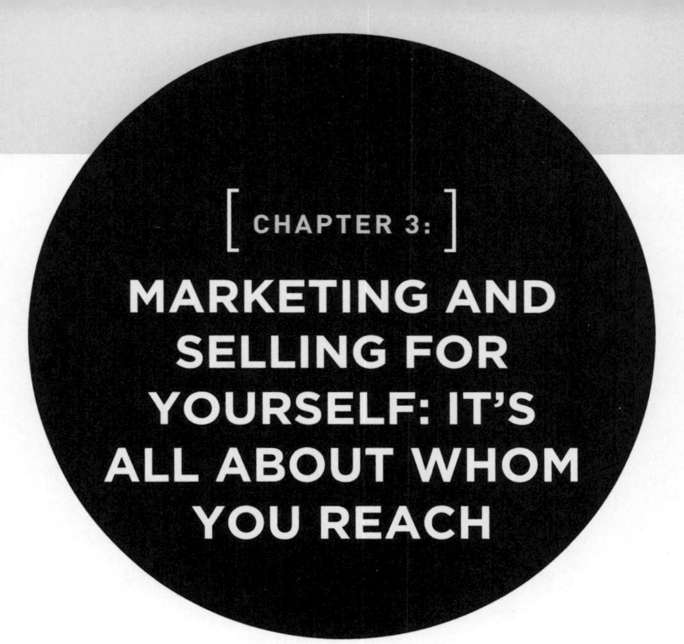

[CHAPTER 3:] MARKETING AND SELLING FOR YOURSELF: IT'S ALL ABOUT WHOM YOU REACH

The blunt truth is that you won't get very far without using effective marketing and selling techniques. "Selling" doesn't necessarily mean offering a physical product: you can sell your services, your insight and advice, and many other things. But in order for people to buy what you're offering, you have to let them know you exist. And this can seem like a constant uphill struggle. It's true: marketing never ends, and even when you've hit a plateau and scored some real successes, you'll already have to be thinking about the next marketing campaign. This chapter will give you some of the basics for both marketing and selling, though it's not comprehensive. For more in-depth studies of each topic, see *This Book Will Teach You Marketing Fundamentals* and *This Book Will Teach You Essential Sales Strategies*, also in this series.

WHAT IS MARKETING?

This is the big question! Marketing is actually many things, but it's also simple to define, sort of. And of course, the more you get involved with the subject, the more complex and never-ending it gets! You may be new to marketing, and that's fine. This chapter will introduce you to some key concepts and actions to take that will give you a start on what will likely be a life-long journey.

The American Marketing Association defines marketing as the "activity, set of institutions, and processes for creating, communicating, delivering, and exchanging offerings that have value for customers, clients, partners, and society at large," which is as good an introductory definition as any. When marketing, you are trying to establish yourself and your brand as a solid and quality provider of a product or service that others will want and pay you for. At the same time, you want to be cultivating relationships with clients and customers, so that you will both benefit.

At its most basic, good marketing takes into account needs, wants, and demands.

- **Needs:** These are what people must have for everyday living and to feel secure. They include food and water, clothing, and shelter, as well as psychological needs such as feeling loved, safe, accepted, included, and valued. They are both physical and intangible, and have great importance in people's lives.

- **Wants:** Wants are not strictly necessary (despite what some might say!), but can bring happiness and satisfy a lot of those same psychological cravings, even if only for a while. Marketing is very much as focused on wants as it is on needs, and for some, the line between the two may be blurred! Wants are influenced by our own psychological profile, our environment, what our friends and families think, advertising and media, and a host of other factors.

- **Demands:** Demands are what arises when there is either a need or a want, and a customer has the ability to claim it. In most cases, this means the ability to pay. Advertising often tries to make a want seem like a need, in order to convince a target market to make the purchase. If someone thinks they "need" the latest model of a phone, they will "demand" it.

"You shouldn't focus on why you can't do something, which is what most people do. You should focus on why perhaps you can, and be one of the exceptions."

— STEVE CASE (COFOUNDER OF AOL)

DOING MARKET RESEARCH

In order to find out what your potential markets want and need, you'll need to conduct some fairly extensive research. This can seem boring, overwhelming, and unnecessary, but it's not a step you can skip, if you really want to connect with potential clients and customers. You have to know who they are and what they're looking for, so you can best fulfill their wants and needs. You'll need to do research at both the primary and secondary levels to get a good sense of what you need to offer.

- **Secondary research:** This will be the best place for you to begin, because it's easier. In secondary research, you'll be looking at existing data. This is great, because the work has already been done for you. You want to be looking for information about markets anywhere that might be useful: magazines, blogs, online articles, sales figures, company reports, etc. Anywhere you think might give you some insight into your potential target market(s) will be a good place to start. Another great point to begin with is to look at your potential competition. What are they doing that you might be able to do better? What you want to be looking for, simply put, is: Does one market (or more) exist for what you want to do? Hopefully, the answer is yes, but if not, you may have to go back to your original plan and revise it until you can make it work. Once you have a market, you'll need to move on to doing some primary research.

- **Primary research:** Obviously, this is information gathering that you'll have to conduct yourself. As such, it will be unique to you and potentially far more useful. Here are some of the options you can choose from:

- **Surveys:** Surveys and questionnaires are a great way to get quick and valuable feedback. Companies use them all the time, and you've no doubt filled out countless forms for these information requests in the past. In general, the more people you can survey, the better, since you'll get a broader selection of the population and a wider range of answers.

- **Interviews:** Think of an interview as a very focused survey. You can hear from someone exactly what they want and what they don't want. Obviously, interviews are more time-consuming and hard to set up, and you can't get as many responses as you could from a bigger and broader survey or questionnaire. But if you really want to get some clear answers from a small sampling of your potential target market, they can be a great way to go.

- **Focus groups:** A focus group is essentially a bigger group interview. The idea is to bring together a sampling of your target market to a single location, often just a room, sitting around a table. In recent years more focus groups have also taken place online. The idea is to have a moderator ask them questions. The group setting and team spirit might produce more interesting answers, as someone could bring up something the others had not yet thought of. You'll normally want to compensate people for their time, however, so be mindful of that if you're on a budget.

- **Field trials:** When you're getting near to launching your product or service, this kind of research can be very helpful. The idea is to test out, say, an advertisement, and see what kind of response it gets. You may want to try more than one version, to see which one receives the best response. Or maybe you have two potential ways of delivering a service, and want to see which one is more efficient. You can have a group of volunteers try out each for free and see which one gets the better reaction.

"No research is ever quite complete."

—MERVIN GORDON

FINDING THE RIGHT MARKET: SIX METHODS

Sorry to say, but not everyone is going to want what you're offering, even if it seems like perfect fit. People have brand loyalties that sometimes can't be overcome. They will always buy the latest phone from Apple, or they'll always buy a certain type of shoes, and nothing you offer is going to get them to change their minds. So, accept that you can't be everything to everyone, and focus instead on markets that *will* be receptive to your message; sometimes that means the smaller, the better. Here are some suggestions for narrowing down your target markets to a realistic and reachable size.

1. **Use what you already have on your current customers.** This only works if you actually *have* current customers, of course. But if you do, go back and research them. How did they find you? What demographic are they in? What marketing worked best to bring them around to you? If you're doing some things right, you need to be doing more of those things.

2. **Examine what are you actually offering.** Obviously, you know what you're offering! But think about whom it's going to serve. Who really wants and needs what you're selling? It's not enough to have a great product or service. Others have to see that it's

great and feel that they want or need it. How can you match your offerings with the people that will most appreciate them? Don't waste time on demographics that aren't in the main target; you're not likely to win them over. Having a niche market is fine, if it's sustainable. Offering something that only twenty-three people in the world want isn't going to work, though!

3. **Look at psychographics.** Psychographics are not the same as demographics. They refer to more intangible things like personalities, habits and customs, interests, lifestyles, and opinions. They cover how your customers think and feel, which as you can imagine, can be very influential over how they buy. You need to understand the "why" of your customers, so that you can effectively sell to them. Psychographics can be gleaned from surveys and questionnaires, focus groups, interviews, and so on. Let your potential base speak for itself, and listen.

4. **Look at social media analytics.** Use the data analysis tools of various social media sites. These can tell you who's looking at your page(s). If they're already following or liking your page, it shows they're interested.

5. **Ask who is in your competitors' target groups.** It's very useful to see whom your competitors are going after for their own businesses. Some will potentially be in the same group, but some will probably be different. Is there anything in those different groups that you could appeal to, to bring them over to your side? Can you offer them something they're not getting that would convince them to switch brands?

6. **Never stop reassessing your target markets.** As with so much of this process, it's ongoing, and you'll always be returning to it to figure out ways to improve it. Your market might change over time; maybe some of them will grow out of a need for your service or products (this is

especially true if you market to specific age groups, such as babies and children). Your product may be really popular one year, and not so much the next year. This is the risk of running your own business. Your customers and clients will come and go, even the loyal ones, so always be ready to redefine your message and adapt.

> **"If you can offer a free tier that provides a lot of value, it will naturally help your product to spread much more rapidly."**
>
> ***—MELANIE PERKINS (COFOUNDER OF CANVA)***

DEVELOPING A MARKETING PLAN: NINE STEPS

Just as with your business plan, you'll need a marketing plan. In fact, your marketing plan should be a part of your overall business plan. Any investors that you approach will want to see what you have in mind to let the world know you exist. There is certain information your plan should have, outlined here.

1. **Define your goals.** What do you want to achieve with this marketing campaign? Just saying "sell more products or services" isn't enough. You need to narrowly define each goal, the amount of time it will take to reach it, and what purpose it will serve. Not every goal needs to be huge, but everything should serve the larger goal of getting your name out there. And this will allow you to keep an eye on your progress.

2. **Create your summary.** Go back to your business plan and use it as a guide to define yourself, who you are, and what you do. Some suggest doing the SWOT analysis, which refers to your business's Strengths, Weaknesses, Opportunities, and Threats: What's good about your business, what needs to be improved, what opportunities do you have, and what could cause you problems?

3. **Identify your markets.** Whatever information you have gathered so far on your markets, include it here. You may have more than one market, which is fine, even great! But consider that you may have to use

different strategies to reach them, especially if they are separated by something substantial, such as age or geography (see below).

4. **Develop your strategies.** Now that you know whom you'll be reaching out to, it's time to think about how you'll do it. Which media will be most effective in reaching out to your various markets? Is one preferable in one group, but not in another? Are there methods that will work across all groups? This process will probably take some real time and research, and is probably the most important step in your plan, so pay close attention to it. You don't want to waste money on ineffective marketing methods.

5. **Identify your competition.** You probably already know who your closest competitors are, but if you haven't yet looked too much into them, now is the time to do it. You need to see what they offer versus what you do, and what you might offer as a better alternative.

6. **Include your budget.** Your budget is crucial to making the whole thing work. You must have an amount set aside for paying for your marketing, and it's very important that you know what your upper spending limit is in each category you've chosen to try out. Marketing and advertising can get very expensive very quickly, and you can waste a lot of money on ineffective methods if you haven't done your homework. See the next section for more details on developing a budget.

7. **Keep everyone informed.** If you are a sole proprietor, then you're good to go. But if you have partners or investors, you must keep them in the loop, and this plan must be shared. All partners need to agree on it, and if there are any disagreements, you'll need to get those worked out in advance. Never launch into a marketing and advertising campaign if anyone has reservations or concerns.

8. **Use builder and driver campaigns.** Builder campaigns, as the name suggests, build toward something in the long term. They recur: think social media posts, newsletters, blogs, and so on. They remind people on a regular basis that you're out there and doing great things. They also can be quite inexpensive, unless you pay to boost your presence on social media sites. They're a great place to start, and everyone should use them regularly. Driver campaigns are meant to be shortterm, usually focused on a single event, such as a product launch, an event, or some other finite occurrence. You can use your builder campaigns to advertise these as well, but a driver campaign will be focused solely on the upcoming happening. This is where you'll more likely be spending money.

9. **Make it work!** Put together a plan of action to set everything in motion, and stick to it! You'll want a calendar with deadlines and to-do lists to keep you on track. Enlist the help of others, if you need to, in order to stick with it.

"The will to win is worthless if you do not have the will to prepare."

—THANE YOST

FOUR POINTS FOR CREATING A MARKETING BUDGET

Just as you have an overall budget for your company, it's essential to include in that a budget for marketing and advertising. Unless you can achieve success by word-of-mouth advertising alone (not likely, but please write a book about how to do it if you can!), you'll have to do some fairly serious shouting to get attention. How much you can spend will of course depend on your overall budget, the size of your business, and the type of marketing you'll need to do. But even on a small budget, you can do quite well, if you follow this advice given here.

1. **Know your overall budget.** You'll have to be sure about your company's finances, even if you're just getting started. It may be tempting to allocate a significant amount to marketing to get yourself off the ground, but if you misuse your funds, all of the good marketing in the world won't prevent your business from failing. Start smaller and work your way up. You may have to wait until you have some revenue or other funding before you can really launch the marketing campaign you want to, but that's better than spending too much at the start and not getting enough value for it. Even if you think you have the greatest product ever (hint: you don't), be wise about your spending. If it's truly that great, word will get out.

2. **Spend your money wisely.** Choose carefully where you want to spend your money. Your budget will likely be limited, so be strategic and try to spread your money around to the most useful areas. Spending it all in one place will be a disaster, so forget about the full-page newspaper or magazine ad; you're not there yet! Look at things like online ads, boosted posts on social media, press releases (free), and so on. Aim to get your message out more widely, not more loudly, at least not at first. Your focus should be on the internet, where so much commerce happens. That's not to say that some traditional sources can't be good, but again, consider the type of business you have and what best suits it. If your potential clientele is mostly older, then you might be able to focus a bit more on traditional media, but if your base is almost all under thirty, online and social media are the way to go. Some things you try won't work, but you'll learn as you go—all the more reason not to blow large amounts on untested methods!

3. **Choose your options wisely.** It's going to be necessary to try different strategies, to see what gets the best response. But be careful about going with anything too wild and unusual, at least at the start. Unless you have an unorthodox idea that is really tied into your overall business, stay with methods and techniques that have been proven to work for a while. You'll need to gather some data on how effective your early campaigns are, and from there you can try new and less conventional ideas. If your target market responds well to one particular method of marketing, it's a sign that you're doing the right thing.

4. **Keep an eye on competitors and the industry.** What in general seems to be working in your industry? Do you have a competitor who is succeeding by doing one kind of marketing? Look into why. You won't know their budget, of course, but you might be able to estimate the cost and get a sense of what it would cost you to try something similar. Obviously, you don't want to just slavishly copy what the competition is doing; you need your own voice. But if certain forms of marketing (print vs. online, radio vs. podcast, etc.) seem to work in your industry, that's an indication of where you should spend your money.

CREATING YOUR WEBSITE: SEVEN THINGS TO REMEMBER

You can't afford to be without a website these days; it's where people will come if they're responding well to your marketing efforts. And it needs to be well designed, professional looking, and accessible across all devices, from desktops to phones. It's your online calling card, your brochure that tells the world about you and the fantastic services or products that you offer. If you've never had one, or if you're retrofitting a site from 2002, don't worry. It's never been easier to get a good site up and running quickly! Here are some things to keep in mind.

1. **Make sure that it looks professional.** This is critical. An old HTML-based design from the early 2000s just won't cut it anymore. It needs to be clear, easy to navigate, and present everything that you need to present. Skip the self-loading video and audio: people hated this back in the 1990s, and they still hate them now, even though they've made a comeback for some strange reason! The good news is, there are countless excellent website templates available now, and many build-it-yourself designs that make the whole process a lot easier than it was even a few years ago. If you're feeling creative, dive in and see what you can do on your own. If you're still apprehensive, hire someone to do it for you; it's a worthwhile investment!

2. **It's all about SEO.** You've probably heard of SEO and SEM. "Search Engine Optimization" is a big buzzword these days. Everyone wants it; everyone is clamoring for it. It's a selling point that freelance designers and writers offer. And at its most basic, it's not a difficult concept. It simply means the use of keywords that allow your website to show up higher in search engine rankings. It's a way of making sure that if people use a search engine to look for something you offer, your page will come up at the top or close to it in the results, thus increasing the chances that this potential customer will visit your site. It's a form of marketing that seeks to place you in front of potential targets without having to do anything other than make sure that it's all set up beforehand. If you're using a designer, they'll likely understand this and work to include important words and terms in your metadata. Try to use words that are directly related to your business; you'll need several—and the more specific you can make them, the better. Just adding "clothing" or "software" won't get you good results.

3. **Keep your site updated.** Always make sure that your site is current and sees regular activity. You've undoubtedly been to websites where the last update was six months ago, a year ago, even more? How did that make you feel about the business? Probably not that great. If they can't be bothered, why should you? Don't be that business.

4. **Have a blog.** One of the simplest ways to keep your site up-to-date is to blog regularly. As with social media, you can post items that your base will be interested in and some periodic updates on what you're up to. It doesn't have to be a long essay; in fact, it's better if it isn't. Make sure also that this information is easily shareable on social media and other sites, so that your biggest fans can easily spread the word. This is great social proof, and it lets your enthusiasts do the work for you by getting your site in front of their friends and contacts.

5. **Give something away.** One way to make your website fun and interactive is to offer something for free to your potential clients and customers. This doesn't have to be anything elaborate, but it should have genuine value. Maybe it's a small free sample or a two-page report in a downloadable PDF. Usually, the best practice is to offer this in exchange for the person's email. You've no doubt seen this countless times on your own journeys around the internet. They give you their email for your mailing list, and get the bonus. Of course, they might just unsubscribe after they get what they came for, but a good number won't.

6. **Always give value.** Don't waste your potential customers' time on your site by making it hard to explore or overladen with junk that's not relevant to them. There's a running joke about cooking blogs that have to put a personal essay about their Italian grandmother before each recipe, so that you have to scroll down through endless amounts of text to get to the actual recipe itself. In this case, it's done for copyright reasons, but it's taken on a horrid life of its own. Don't be a cooking blog. Get to the point, and give your visitors what they came for. Tell your story, yes, but keep personal histories confined to one page. Instead, put in things like reviews and testimonials, and scatter them around the site.

7. **Be contactable.** Always, always make it easy to be reached. Put whatever information you're comfortable sharing on the site, and give it a dedicated page that can be clicked right at the top. You'll sometimes see big companies with a contact option only at the bottom of a long scroll on the landing page. They're saying they don't want you to contact them, and if they're behaving like that, why would you?

MARKETING WITH TRADITIONAL MEDIA

Despite the internet ruling everything these days, there is still much value in looking at traditional forms of media to get your message out. This is especially true if you run a local business such as a restaurant, small shop, or bookstore. National advertising may be beyond your reach (and you probably won't need it for a while anyway), but local advertising and marketing with these methods still offers some great opportunities to get noticed.

RADIO

The glory days of radio are long gone, but it still remains a powerful force for communication. With over nine hundred radio stations of all different kinds (traditional, digital, internet, etc.) across Canada in multiple languages, there's great potential to reach target audiences. Studies have suggested that about two-thirds of Canadians who work full-time have some kind of radio on while working, which gives you many excellent opportunities to be heard. It's estimated that nearly one-third of our media time is spent listening to radio, so it's well worth considering.

With radio, you have various choices:

- **Analog:** Traditional stations are still going strong. The CBC is the largest, of course, and discussions are ongoing about advertising there, with some movement to make the CBC ad-free. In addition, you can look at options like college campus radio (which does have restrictions on how many

hours of advertising can be broadcast each week) and community radio (which generally doesn't have such restrictions). Start researching individual stations and their programs to see where you might be a good fit.

- **SiriusXM Radio Canada:** The Canadian affiliate of SiriusXM Radio, it currently offers about 130 channels and claims to have over sixty-five million listeners. However, studies have shown that ad-free radio is a much more popular format, so be careful about anyone selling you ad space and making bold promises about the number of people you'll reach.

- **Internet:** Many traditional stations also have online versions, which allows their broadcasts to be heard worldwide. The popularity of streaming radio is on the rise; estimates show that the average Canadian now listens to up to seven hours of streamed radio per week. It may be worth investigating if it's something you want to get in on.

- **General advice:** Research the kinds of shows that your target markets and demographics likely listen to. Ask the radio station in question. Run your ads during those shows and do so daily, or at least several times a week. Repeat airings will help get your message across. Just one airing will do nothing. Be patient; it often takes a few months to really see make an impact and get results. Bear that in mind when crafting a potential radio budget.

TELEVISION

Television advertising can be more effective, but of course, it will cost a lot more than radio ads. When you're starting out, your budget may not be able to accommodate the expenses, and a good TV ad could be something to shoot for when you've got more of a reputation. With over eight hundred television channels across Canada (with more being added), there is potential to be seen and heard, and in most cases you'll be looking at local and regional channels, not national ones.

- **Local stations:** These will be your most likely targets as a newer business. Many are affiliates of networks, but also offer their own programming tailored to local audiences. There could be some good options here if your business is locally focused.

- **National stations:** These include CBC, CTV, Global, Ici Radio-Canada Télé, TVA, and Omni Television. At least for a while, these will be out of your budget, and may never be appropriate for the kind of business you're running anyway. You'll need the assistance of an advertising agency or similar professional service to make sure the contracts are clear. Again, this is all probably not necessary when you're starting out.

- **General advice:** Just as with radio, you need to choose your time slots carefully, targeting your ads to audiences that watch specific programs and are likely to be more receptive to them. Given the cost, it won't be feasible to run an ad at the same time every day for months, so you'll have to make it good and make it count. Be aware that your contract will have you locked in for at least a certain amount of time, so budget accordingly. The station will probably have demographic information that can be useful. Some stations will offer to produce an ad for you, which can be helpful if you don't have the equipment or can't afford to hire a company to make the ad, but these vary widely in quality, so be careful!

NEWSPAPERS

Physical newspapers are still a thing, especially among older demographics, and if your products or services target them, these can be a great way to get your message out. Given that most papers also have online versions, doing an online ad campaign may be a great and affordable option, getting your ad out quickly and in front of a lot of readers.

Check out *Newspapers Canada* (see Resources, on page 153) for a great online resource to learn more about the Canadian newspaper industry.

- **Local papers:** There are more than one thousand community papers across Canada, said to publish sixteen million copies of their editions each week. Recent research shows that nearly three-quarters of Canadians in more rural areas read their community papers on a regular basis. These papers are usually free, and rely on advertising to keep going. So, depending on your business, you could have a great source for advertising and also help keep a valued community resource going by regularly advertising with them. Again, many of these papers have online versions. Something else to bear in mind: local papers need stories, so why not reach out and pitch a story about your new business? See if someone will write a feature or an interview about you and what you're offering. It's something that is community news, and it's fantastic free advertising that allows you to go into much more detail about your story.

- **National papers:** National papers such as the *Globe and Mail*, *Toronto Star*, and *Le Journal de Montreal* continue to have large print circulations (in the hundreds of thousands). Nearly two dozen other national newspapers across the country have circulations between 30,000 and 180,000. If you are ready to take you message to a larger audience, a national paper is a good way to go. Bear in mind that they also have online versions, which may be a better option, since those will likely endure, even as readership slowly declines for physical papers over the years.

- **General advice:** Your ad needs to stand out. In a physical paper, you probably won't have much say over where it's placed, so it needs to get people's attention, whatever your budget. But you don't want to make it garish! Work with a designer who knows how to craft quality ads that grab people's attentions. Don't let the paper do the design for you, if it offers. You know how you want to be represented, and you're in charge. If you give up that control, you might get something that's not you at all! Use your ad to describe the benefit of what you offer, keep the message brief (people don't have the time or interest in reading wordy ads), don't waste space bragging about yourself (unless it's a very short testimonial), and make sure to include some kind of call to action in the ad. This can be something like "visit our website to claim your free gift now!" or "call now for more exciting details." You want to get the reader to do something in response, so make it enticing.

MAGAZINES

Magazines, even in print form, don't seem to be going away anytime soon. *Magazines Canada* (see Resources on page 153) reports that the largest demographic for reading magazines is the age range of eighteen to twenty-four, with twenty-five to thirty-four and thirty-five to forty-nine following close behind. Some 80 percent of magazines are consumer-oriented, while the other 20 percent are trade magazines. Don't neglect the trades when you are looking at magazine advertising, if there are magazines devoted to your industry. These can be prime locations to get yourself noticed. As with papers, a good number of magazines have online versions, though (also like papers), many are behind paywalls and accessible by subscription only.

That can actually be good, since subscribers already have an interest in the magazine's topics, and if your ad dovetails with their interests, they'll probably be more receptive to it.

- **Local and regional magazines:** As with other traditional media, these will probably be your best bet at first. It's fair to say there's probably a magazine for everyone, even if it only exists online. As with local papers, magazines need interesting stories, so if you're launching your business or if you've hit an important landmark at six months, why not reach out to one or more and see if they'll do a story on you? It's a great form of free advertising, and maybe you can also pay for an ad in the same edition, to help drive home your message?

- **National magazines:** Like national papers, these may be out of your reach and budget for some time, and that's OK. Advertising in these kinds of periodicals can get very expensive. Again, it may be worth your time to explore doing some online ads, if it's a magazine directly related to your industry and you can conduct business on a national scale. They're probably less interested in doing a story about you, unless you are really doing something creative and innovative, but it doesn't hurt to reach out and ask.

- **General advice:** Use the same procedures for newspapers with magazines, since there is a definite overlap. You may have a bit more control over where the ad is placed. Obviously, if you've bought space on the inside covers or back cover, you know exactly where it will go, but of course, these will be much more expensive. Since the magazine is (probably?) in color, you'll have some more control over the design, which can make the ad more attractive. Again, make sure it's professionally designed; you need it to make a great impression.

THE MANY TYPES OF (INTERNET) MARKETING

Fortunately, when it comes to the vast and bewildering world of the internet, you have many options for marketing your new business, and they are accessible and relatively easy to understand and get started with. You can pick and choose what seems best for you, and try out different options to see which bring the best results.

- **Content Marketing:** Content marketing is a way of providing value to your base. It isn't about selling your wares; it's about giving your customers and clients information and other content—for free—that will help them, and build your reputation as an authority and a trustworthy source. Think of a bank or investment service that sends out a monthly email newsletter with financial advice and investing tips. They're giving this information away, and they're not trying to sell anything. Rather, they're presenting themselves as a trusted source, and over time, subscribers will probably decide to come to them for their other needs. This sort of marketing is a great way to reach out to your base and make them feel valued. You can customize this kind of marketing to almost any business, and it's well worth taking the time to do so. Offering information and other content of genuine value will come back to you in sales and loyalty over time.

- **Affiliate Marketing:** Affiliate marketing is a way of letting others do the marketing for you; great, right? Essentially, others advertise your products and services (say, on their website), and for each sale that you make through them, they earn a commission. The more sales they bring to you, the more they make, the more you make, and everyone wins! The fact is that most people aren't going to get rich being affiliates, and many scam websites and how-to's take advantage of people's wishful thinking. But if you have a customer who genuinely believes in what you produce, it might be worth investigating a partnership, even if you both only have limited sales this way.

- **Newsletters:** An email newsletter is pretty much a must. It's a fantastic way to keep in touch with your target markets and let them know what's up in your world. As mentioned earlier, an easy way to grow your mailing list is to offer something of value to your website visitors in exchange for them signing up to receive your emails. Of course, they can always opt out at any time, so there's no real pressure. Just make sure that you don't only use your email list to sell things, and be careful about posting too often. If you do either of these things, your recipients are likely to get annoyed and unsubscribe. Be sensitive to their needs. How much email do you still get daily? And have you experienced the situation where you signed up for a mailing list, only to receive something every day? You got tired of it real fast, didn't you? So don't be that company.

- **Blogs:** Like a newsletter, a blog is something you should invest the time in having. It's a way of keeping your website updated regularly, and like a newsletter, it should offer your readers something of value. You don't need to compose a lengthy essay every few days. A short note with a link to an interesting article, an informative video about trends, or a new book by an industry leader are all ways of populating your blog without it getting too sales-y. Of course, once in a while, you can use it to promote your products and services, or brag if you've done something amazing, just don't make that the whole purpose of it. You can use your newsletter to link to your blog posts, and you should definitely advertise it regularly on your social media pages. Make sure you put things in your blog that your readers can't get elsewhere; it will entice them to come back regularly and subscribe.

- **Search Engine Optimization (SEO):** As noted above, everything is about SEO these days, for better and worse. It seems like it's all you hear about, and it definitely is important. Having the right keywords will help you get your site close to the top of searches, but you need to be strategic about it. If in doubt (and it is a complex and sometimes confusing topic), seek out the help of a writer or web designer with expertise in how to do it.

- **Influencers:** Opinions are divided on this method of marketing, but it might be something you can explore, depending on the nature of your business. But if someone famous (or relatively so) likes your product or service and uses it, it's worth reaching out to them to see if they will tell their fans and followers about it. If so, you've just greatly expanded your market! An endorsement of your offering to that person's fans has a lot of social proof built into it. It's likely that their followers will also be interested in what you sell, simply by association. If you hear about someone who could be of help, try contacting them. To be honest, they may not do it for free, and why should they? If a company asked them to do a commercial for their product (and that's pretty much what this is), they would expect to be paid. So, you may not be able to get a famous movie star, but someone on YouTube or Instagram with a hefty number of followers might well be willing to give you a shout-out. Celebrity endorsements are never going away!

- **Paid Advertising:** Of course, you can get your message out to the world by paying for it—the old-fashioned way! The downside is that people hate ads and often tend to ignore them; there's a reason why ad-blocking programs are so popular. So you need to investigate whether it's worth your time, or if you're just throwing your money away. It will take some definite

strategic thinking about when and where you place your online ads, and you need to be mindful of your budget, since the cost of online advertising can add up quickly.

You might consider paid search ads, where the link to your business appears at the top of a search, marked with "ad." Of course, many people will ignore these, simply because they're noted as such. You can also pay to appear in social media feeds, but again, these are sometimes seen negatively by users, and an ad-blocking program will tend to filter them out. Another method is native advertising, which makes use of sponsored articles about companies and products, which are placed into the normal rotation of a site's articles. And there are the much-maligned display ads that appear at the sides of pages, and invite you to click them. None of these are necessarily bad, but they all have drawbacks. To use them effectively, you'll have to do research on what works and doesn't. Remember that in these days of privacy concerns, people don't like ads that are targeted to them based on their search histories. It feels invasive and might make people react negatively to your business.

MARKETING WITH SOCIAL MEDIA

Social media is an indispensable tool for marketing, whether one likes it or not. Your business will almost certainly need to have a presence on Facebook, Twitter, and perhaps other sites, to give you the chance to reach more potential customers and clients. You don't necessary have to be on all of them; the nature of your business will determine your needs. If your target groups are primarily older customers, for example, you probably don't need to be on Snapchat or even Instagram. Analytics can give you a look into who's viewing your pages. Use these sites as tools to help you, but don't be ruled by them. Much of the information on networking for Facebook, Twitter, and LinkedIn also applies to marketing (see "Networking Online with Social Media" on page 56). This section will focus on some of the other alternatives, such as YouTube, Instagram, Snapchat, and Pinterest.

- **YouTube:** Depending on your business, YouTube can be a valuable tool for getting your message out, but you need to keep in mind several things:
    - **Have a clear goal:** Why are you on YouTube? What is the message you're trying to promote? It does no good to have a YouTube channel for the sake of having one. What, specifically, are you promoting with your videos?

- **Post regularly:** As with other platforms, just posting once every three months will get you nowhere. Have a regular posting schedule and stick to it. If you want to gather a group of subscribers, you'll need to keep them engaged with regular content, even if the videos are brief. Don't just post to post; make your videos useful.

- **Keep the quality high:** You need to make sure that the video and audio quality of your content is good. You can't afford to look cheap or lazy. If you're serious about using YouTube, you'll probably need to invest in some good camera equipment, and maybe in creating a background set that looks appealing.

- **Use keywords and links:** As with other platforms, keywords are essential so that you come up in searches, and they need to match the content of each individual posting. Always link back to your website or blog so that interested viewers can find out more.

- **Respond to your viewers:** Take the time to answer questions, thank them, and contribute to conversations in the comments.

- **Forget about going viral:** Sure, it may happen, but put your energy into developing a solid and loyal following. If they like what you're posting, they'll share it.

• **Instagram:** Instagram can be surprisingly useful as a means of marketing, especially if you have products for sale. Here are some tips:

- **Post regularly:** Even more so with this platform, have a posting schedule and stick to it. You might be able to do so every day, but even if it's just three days a week, post on the same three days at approximately the same times. You probably don't need to post more than once or twice a day at the start; that could change if your business really takes off.

- **Use your home page wisely:** You can only post one link, so it needs to be important. It may just be to your website, or if you're posting about interesting news or other products, you may be changing it regularly. Direct viewers to your home page in your posts, since the link in them will not be "hot."

- **Use hashtags:** They are essential on Instagram, so it's OK to use more of them. That way you can fine-tune your post and potentially reach larger numbers of people.

- **Post only relevant topics and images:** Again, don't post just to post. Make your posts pertinent to your business, or at least interesting to your followers. If you don't have enough to post daily, do it every other day. What matters more is that it's regular and relevant.

• **Snapchat:** Though geared toward younger users, Snapchat is actually very popular with age ranges into the mid-thirties, so it could be a useful tool for you.

  - **Post often:** Since posts only last for twenty-four hours, you're going to need to have more of a presence here if you want to be noticed. If that's too much of a commitment for you, Snapchat probably isn't for you.

  - **Create a sponsored filter or lens:** Details are on the site. Snapchat is great for funny posts, and you can use humor to be more engaging with your followers. If there is anything lighthearted about your business, you might be able to use that to your advantage here.

  - **Encourage followers to engage:** If you have a product, invite followers to share a post about how they use it. Include these in your own stories, and let your fans market for you!

  - **Keep your stories short:** As with the short life span of posts, don't put up lengthy posts. People want things to be short and sweet.

- **Consider not using sound all the time:** It can be a useful tool, but not everyone viewing posts on their phones has their sound up. If your post relies entirely on sound for its message, it's going to be lost on a portion of viewers.

- **Stay on topic:** Fun is fun, but be careful and remember that you're still a business. Engage your demographic with fun posts, but make them relevant. It's fine to be spontaneous and not worry about perfection here. It gives you a chance to show your human side.

• **Pinterest:** Perhaps surprisingly, many businesses use Pinterest very effectively. It's especially good if you are selling multiple products, like a clothing line. Here are some ideas:

- **Post good quality images:** If you want people to see what you're selling, they have to be able to see it! Don't skimp on this or post low-res photos. You need to show yourself off at your best.

- **Pin regularly:** You should pin every day, if you can. It's fine to pin other content, but make it related to your business and what you do. Consider using rich pins, which give real-time information.

- **Fill out your boards:** If you leave them empty, it doesn't send a great message. Who wants to look at a profile that can't be bothered to provide content?

- **Have different boards for different subjects:** Don't just put everything on one board. It looks cluttered and messy, and is harder to navigate. Think about your viewers and what they might want. Make it easy for them.

- **Keep hashtags to a minimum:** Unlike Instagram, minimal use of hashtags will work better for you. Make them count, so that people can search for you.

THE BASICS OF SELLING

You already know what selling is. But there may be more to it than you're aware of. At its simplest, it's a transaction between the seller and the buyer. The buyer offers something, usually money, in exchange for a product or service that they need or want. The seller tries to convince the buyer that their offering is what the buyer is looking for. Both parties should be satisfied with the transaction, and both should feel that good value was given and received. Here are some details that you probably know, at least vaguely, but it's good to have them laid out clearly.

- **Selling products and services:** Businesses are most often engaged in the selling of one of these two things. It's also quite common for a business to sell both. A store may sell computers (a product) but offer an additional three-year warranty (a service) for an extra cost. A health coach may sell their service (advising) but also offer a cookbook or an exercise video (a product) that goes along with their service, again for an extra cost. Of course, many businesses only offer one of these two choices. A business consultant or a lawyer is probably only offering a service, while a florist only sells flowers. Whatever the nature of your business, you'll no doubt see how these things are different but overlap.

- **Selling other things:** It's also possible to sell other things. A freelancer sells their expertise and services, but these are usually for a short time, say a two-month contract to write an engineering manual or a week to design a website. They can "resell" these services to the same client in the future, as the need arises. You may be selling an idea or "selling" your company to a potential investor. You're "selling" yourself at a job interview. If you work for a charity, you may be selling the organization to potential donors. All of these situations require strategies and the ability to convince the "customer" that parting with money or taking you on will be beneficial to you both.

- **Various kinds of markets:** In most cases, you'll probably be selling goods or services, so here is a quick overview of the different types of markets: consumer, industrial, and reseller. You may engage in business in one or more of them, depending on what you offer. You may sell bread at your local bakery but also provide it to the local grocery stores, for example. Or you may sell auto parts to the general public, but also have a contract with a local shipping company to outfit their trucks.

  - **Consumer:** This is the market with which you'll probably be most familiar, the market for everything from tires to toothpaste. These are things that consumers need, that the general public buys. Services would include lawyers, accountants, gardeners, etc. If the people buy it, it's part of the consumer market.

  - **Industrial:** This is the market for other businesses. Companies buy your products and services to help them produce their own products and services or to help them run their day-to-day affairs. Machine parts, mainframes, medical equipment, air conditioners—these are all things that a business might need. A service to a company might be as a business architect or a lawyer.

  - **Reseller:** This is the middleman market. A store gets its stock from suppliers and in turn sells it on their shelves for more than they bought it. A wholesaler buys items at a significant discount in large quantities and sells them for more. An outlet store gets end-of-run clothing and sells it at a discount.

FINDING AND IDENTIFYING POTENTIAL CUSTOMERS

In order to find potential customers, you have to look for them, obviously, but how do you do that? If you've been doing market research, surveys and questionnaires, focus groups, or any other form of digging, you're already well along the way. The process is usually known as prospecting, and like the prospectors of older times, you're looking for gold, in this case those "golden" people who will buy what you're selling. You'll need to cast your net wide and then start getting more focused. As you discover more leads, you'll be dividing them up into two areas: possibilities and prospects. The goal is to convert prospects into customers and clients.

- **Possibilities:** Possibilities are those in your targets that don't yet know much (if anything) about you, but who may be interested in what you offer if they learn enough. These are people that you'll need to reach out to via advertising, word-of-mouth referrals, or your other marketing campaigns. The point is to make a little noise and attract their attention. If you can snag their interest, they may become prospects.

- **Prospects:** Prospects are people (or perhaps other businesses, depending on your ideal clientele), who have learned about you and may have some interest in what you're selling, now or in the future. They haven't bought anything from you yet, but they could, so it's worth cultivating a relationship with them. A prospect is still a prospect until they actually buy from you.

- **Customers and clients:** These two amazing words refer to those who have bought from you. They are beautiful and precious; cherish them! The goal is to give them complete satisfaction so that they go away happy, remain happy, and spread the good word about your fantastic business. With the right kind of relationship building, you can turn one-time buyers into repeat buyers, and those are the true gold that you're prospecting for! You'll be building loyalty to your business and your brand, an amazing thing to have. And it will make your marketing that much easier in the future.

Unfortunately, not everyone is going to want what you have to offer; they just won't, so get used to it, and accept it. It's probably nothing personal (unless you've done something to upset them); it's just that people have an awful lot of choices these days, even in niche markets. So, you need to be clear in your mind about the kinds of customers and clients you need. Here are five ideas on how to do that better.

1. **Do adequate research:** Find out about your target markets and demographics, whether people or businesses. Who are they, really? What do they want and need? How many of them are there (approximately)? How can you best fulfill their wants and needs? Compile the data and make lists.

2. **Get really focused.** Be as specific as you can about your ideal customers. Ask demographic questions, such as age range, economic status, where they live, what they like and don't like . . . pretty much anything you can do to add more detail is going to help you. If your business is other

businesses, get detailed about what kinds. Where are they located? How many customers do they have? Can you realistically provide what they need in the early stages, or will you need to grow? Maybe you'll want to revisit some companies in a year or two, when you've grown and gotten a reputation.

3. **Identify your ideal customer or client.** Feel free to go wild and imagine the exact, perfect fit. This isn't just about wishing; it's about understanding yourself. Whom are you going to best be able to work with and serve? Who do you think would potentially be difficult? The clearer you can be about the types of people who would be a good match, the more you'll be on the lookout for them. Everyone has to deal with difficult customers at one time or another, but this little exercise may help you minimize some of that and save you headaches later on.

4. **Make sure you have shared values.** This is especially true if you are selling to other companies. Do they represent the things that matter to you? You may think a sale is a sale, but if they are engaging in unethical or even illegal behavior, do you really want your product associated with them? This can also be true of a client-based business. You have every right to pick and choose whom you will take on based on their demeanor and behavior. Having problematic clients will only hurt you later on, especially if there are disputes about pricing or services. It's OK to say no sometimes, if your gut is telling you that something may be wrong. Are you worried that your product might be misused? What can you do to keep that from happening?

5. **Never stop working on your marketing efforts.** As mentioned earlier, marketing is an ongoing task, and you'll get better at it as you go. You always need to be refining how you connect with your audience and potential customers and clients. Methods that work for a while may stop working later on, so never get too set in your ways. New customers and clients will always be out there, waiting to hear your message; you just have to find them!

YOU'VE GOT A POTENTIAL CUSTOMER, NOW WHAT? SIX SUGGESTIONS

So, someone is interested in what you do? They may want to buy what you offer. Fantastic, but now what? Don't panic; this is great news! When your marketing is paying off and you're attracting people who are interested in what you do, it means that your work is, well, working. It's what you've been waiting for. Whether you're a coach or consultant, own a store, or have a cool new app, here are some tips for seizing the moment.

1. **Respect the buyer.** Whether it's a person or a company, this buyer deserves your respect and your attention. They've signaled that they may be ready to give you money for what you offer, which means that you have an obligation to get them over the finish line and show them that you are worthy of their trust and their money.

2. **Ask questions.** Find out about them and what they really need. You can't get a good sense of how you can help them if you don't know what they want. It's possible that even they don't quite know what they want! Your task is to help them define it.

3. **Remember, you're selling benefits, not features.** Your potential buyer wants to know what's in it for them, so don't waste their time giving them excruciating details about how your software is built, or what goes into making your shoes. There are some cases where features are a selling point, such as new cars or the new iPhone, but that's because these brands already have a built-in clientele of loyal customers who genuinely want to know what's improved in this year's model. But you're not Apple or BMW, so don't do it.

4. **Answer questions, but don't be on the defensive.** You need to keep control of the conversation and always steer it back to how this product or service will benefit the buyer. It's fine to answer questions, but don't let them direct the conversation.

5. **Overcome objections.** Almost always, a potential customer or client will have objections. Some may seem silly to you, some may be quite valid, but it's important to give your attention to each and never dismiss them. Don't take them personally. They may object about price, timing, actual need, and any number of other things. Your job is to listen to the objection and answer it in a way that validates it but shows that they can get beyond it. If it's about price, stress the value for money. If it's the wrong time, suggest offering some add-ons to sweeten the deal. See the next section for advice on closing, and for a fuller discussion of objections and overcoming them, see *This Book Will Teach You Essential Sales Strategies*, also in this series.

6. **Know when you've said enough.** If the customer says yes, you've done it. You don't need to reassure them that they've made the right choice and that they'll be happy. Too much of this can make a potential buyer suspicious, and maybe even tempt them to back out. It sounds like you're trying to get them to commit before they find out something they don't want to find out. Thank them for the business and be gracious. You can show your appreciation after they are your customer by continuing to value them and checking in, and making right anything that goes wrong.

HOW TO CLOSE THE DEAL

It's an incredible feeling when you actually make a sale. You shake the person's hand, you sign the contract, or maybe you see a happy customer leaving your store, or you get a notification of a sale when someone buys something of yours online that they love. This is what the small business lives for, and it never gets old. But actually making it happen takes the right balance of skills. Here is what you need to know.

Sales happen when several factors come together:

- **What you offer is what they want/need:** This is the first step. You have to be providing what it is they're looking for. If they're not interested, you won't make a sale. Ever. Fortunately, that's why you've done your homework on what target markets to reach out to. They should already be interested.

- **It's the right time for their want/need:** What they want or need is something that has to happen now. Not in two weeks, or next month, but now. And guess what? You can provide it!

- **They value what you have to offer:** They have reviewed what you have to offer and believe that it has value and is worth the price. Your product or service is a quality one.

- **They trust and believe in you:** However you've done it, you have developed a rapport that communicates that you are trustworthy, honest, and want the best for your customers and clients. You're not selling a fraud or a rip-off.

- **They can pay for what they want:** Importantly, they are able to pay for their want/need now. However that takes place (cash, credit, etc.), they can give you your asking price. If they can't, the sale will be delayed and may still fail.

The different ways you can close:

Closing a sale can be done in any number of ways. Here are some of the most common.

- **It's time-sensitive:** Time constraints are great for creating a sense of urgency: "Act now, while supplies last," or "This 25 percent discount will only be good until Friday." These kinds of offers put the pressure on to make a decision sooner rather than later. It can be easy for potential customers to think about it or put it off until next week. Offering a carrot in the form of a time-sensitive enticement often gets people motivated to buy.

- **Offer something in exchange for something:** In this scenario, you offer an additional enticement to get them to buy now. You might throw in a pair of socks if they buy the shirt, but only today. Or you might include two extra coaching sessions at no cost if they sign the contract now. If they ask for something specific, you can also make it conditional on purchasing now.

- **Offer a discount, but give them less.** If the customer is still balking at the price, you can offer to take away a few features and give it to them at the price they want. This is a great way to see how much they really want the whole package.

- **Summarize everything.** Go over the whole deal and the entire product, and show them just what they'll be getting if they act now and buy it. Emphasize the benefits and make it irresistible. This little psychological push may be enough to get them to the sale.

It's fine to use any or all of these in combination, depending on what you're selling. As long as you're being ethical and not trying to defraud them, you're simply helping them along. You want to nudge them without being pushy, and let them buy with total confidence and satisfaction. And that means you have to deliver what you promise and back up everything you say!

NINE WAYS OF ESTABLISHING LONG-LASTING RELATIONSHIPS

It's essential that you build on your customer/client relationships by working to keep them in the long term. New customers are fantastic, and you should always be trying to attract more, but repeat customers are the real gold. These are the loyal ones who value you enough to keep giving you their money, and that's a special thing! The goal is to take single-time-only clients and customers, and convince them to keep coming back to you. Here are some ways that you can strengthen your relationships and make them last.

1. **Check in with them on a regular basis.** It's essential that you keep in touch with your customers and clients. Once a sale is made, that's not the end of things, not by a long shot. It's not enough for them to be on your mailing list and get occasional updates. The following are several ways to keep in touch.

2. **Keep the communication open.** Let your people know that they can reach out to you at any time, for any reason. Make sure that you are easy to contact (again, have it on the website and other material), and be available. Never put off a customer or client!

3. **Show them that you value them.** Let them know that you appreciate their business. They didn't have to choose you, but they did. Don't forget that, and remember that you wouldn't be in business without them.

4. **Always ensure that they're happy.** An unhappy customer or client is a potential disaster. At best, they won't buy from you again; at worst, they leave you a bad review, tell their friends negative stories, and so on. If they're happy today but unhappy two days from now, you'll need to address it.

5. **Ask for feedback and advice.** Ask for comments, send out surveys, solicit opinions, and ask how you can improve. Not everything you get back will be useful, but some of it will be, and if certain answers keep coming back over and over, it's an area you need to look into and work on.

6. **Get back to them.** When someone contacts you, respond as soon as is reasonable. You don't need to email an angry client at midnight, but you should make an effort to reach out to them the following morning during normal business hours. If someone writes or phones asking about what you offer, you have a potential new sale, so give it your attention and enthusiasm, and respond ASAP. They will appreciate your promptness and concern.

7. **Fix any problems right away.** Problems simply cannot stand, no matter what else is going on. If a client is unhappy, you need to do everything reasonable to fix that. Just making that commitment (and letting customers know before something goes wrong) shows that you are responsive to their needs and will work to makes things right. That builds trust.

8. **Let them know you care.** Keep in touch at holidays or other special occasions. Send out a little card (even a virtual one) thanking them for their business. If you have a small client base, a card with a handwritten note is in order. Also, offer useful information in your newsletter or other outgoings. If you have a client with a particular interest and you see something relevant to them, take the time to pass the information along in a personalized email. These kinds of little things go a long way toward building lasting, trusting relationships.

9. **Look for opportunities of mutual benefit.** If you're running a client-based business, consider things that might benefit you both. If your client is a business itself and is doing great things, would it make sense to go in on an ad campaign together? This is known as joint-venture marketing (or advertising), and it could be a great way to advertise what you do to each other's audiences, giving you twice as many potential new customers or clients. Obviously, you'll need to have built up some trust and a relationship already, so as not to appear as if you're using them for your own gain. But if there is a genuine connection there, and a chance for some mutual back-scratching, give it some thought.

[CHAPTER 4:]

LEGAL AND FINANCIAL MATTERS (UGH!)

No matter how cool your idea, product, or service is, the cold, hard reality is that you'll have to deal with the real world sooner rather than later. All of those boring things like tax concerns, legal issues, and many other lovely subjects will force you out of your creative bubble in a hurry. You may fear that you're not good at any of these things. The good news is: you don't have to be. There is a wealth of qualified professionals out there who can assist you in setting up your business the right way, and avoiding any issues early on. This chapter will introduce you to some of the key things you'll need to watch out for, but it should not in any way be considered a substitute for qualified legal or financial advice. When in doubt, seek out the professionals!

THE BORING LEGAL STUFF

Setting up a new business can be anywhere between as easy and as complicated as you want it to be. A sole proprietor has a lot less to deal with at the outset than a corporation, but even there you'll need to do certain things to get your business legally up and running. It isn't actually all that boring, but people usually assume it is! Here are some of the basic steps you need to follow.

- **Register with your province.** You'll need to investigate what you must do with your particular province or territory. In some cases, such as with some simple sole proprietorships, you may not need to register your business at all. In Newfoundland and Labrador, for example, proprietorships or partnerships do not need to register.

- **A federal business number and associated tax accounts.** You may need to acquire these to operate your business; you definitely will if you incorporate. If you are in British Columbia, Manitoba, Nova Scotia, Ontario, or Saskatchewan, you will automatically receive this number when you register. Otherwise, you'll have to apply for it yourself. The Canadian government website gives useful details about these numbers and what they do:

  - **Business number:** a unique, nine-digit number – the standard identifier for businesses. It is unique to a business or legal entity.

- **Canadian Revenue Agency (CRA) program accounts:** Two letters and four digits attached to a business number – used for specific business activities that must be reported to the CRA.

You need a business number if you incorporate or need a CRA program account. You might need a business number to interact with other federal, provincial, and municipal governments in Canada.

When you need CRA program accounts:

Each CRA program account has its own rules and requirements about when you need to register. The most common program accounts a business may need are:

- **GST/HST (RT)** – if your business collects GST/HST [goods and services tax/harmonized sales tax]

- **Payroll deductions (RP)** – if your business pays employees

- **Corporation income tax (RC)** – if your business is incorporated

- **Import-export (RM)** – if your business imports goods or sells goods or services abroad

- **Information returns (RZ)** – if your business files information returns such as tax-free savings account (TFSA), T5, T5013, and more

- **Operating outside of your province or territory.** If you are incorporating, you'll have two choices: to incorporate federally or provincially. Incorporating federally gives you the legal ability to conduct business across Canada, while incorporating provincially only allows you to run your business in your particular province. If you want to operate in other regions, you'll need to register as an extra-provincial or extraterritorial corporation in any jurisdictions beyond your own where you are planning on conducting your business.

- **Permits and licenses.** Depending in the type of business you'll be running, you may need additional permits and/or licenses from federal, provincial, or even municipal authorities. Talk with a business lawyer about your specific situation and needs.

All of this may seem bewildering and overwhelming, so don't freak out! A good accountant will know exactly what you need, based on the type of business that you're planning. But it's good to get a bit familiar with these terms so that you know what's going on and what your obligations will be. This is especially true if you will be hiring anyone to work for you and are planning on growing your business outside of your local area or region.

"My advice is to focus on the importance of forging a long-term relationship, whether with colleagues, partners, or customers. It is often easy to get caught up in short-term decisions."

—SHEILA LIRIO MARCELO (FOUNDER OF CARE.COM)

INTELLECTUAL PROPERTY AND ITS PROTECTION

Depending on the nature of your new business, you may be creating a brand that you want to be recognizable. And if you're developing a brand, you'll want to ensure that it's safeguarded against theft. Logos, designs, and other identifiers are important to your company's identity, and they usually need to be trademarked to protect them against unlawful use. This doesn't mean it won't happen, of course, but you then have the legal standing to take action and shut down any unauthorized use of your logo or designs. If the work you're producing is proprietary (innovative software, for example), you'll also have to look into how to protect it, using everything from nondisclosure agreements to encrypted software. This section gives a brief overview of how you can protect what you produce.

- **Intellectual assets:** These business assets are considered intangible but still have value for your business. According to the Canadian government, these "include inventions, new technologies, new brands, original software, novel designs, unique processes, and much more. These assets have value in the marketplace very much like tangible assets, or assets that you can hold in your hand." And by their very existence, these assets run the risk of being stolen and/or appropriated by competitors or less ethical organizations. It's essential that you protect them, and fortunately, there are many ways of doing so.

- **Copyright:** As the name implies, a copyright gives you the right to produce and reproduce copies of your original work, or substantial parts of it, in any form. These can include art, written works, music, recordings, films and video, software and programs, and many other things. Someone else has the right to use it (such as recording a cover of an original song), but only by paying you for that right.

- **Trademarks:** Trademarks, as defined by the government, are "a combination of letters, words, sounds or designs that distinguishes one company's goods or services from those of others in the marketplace." Famous brand names, famous fictional characters, phrases, and more are often trademarked. Bear in mind that not everything can be trademarked (such as common phrases, words, or clichés), and you'll have to do a thorough search to make sure the identifier you want for your brand is not already being used and is not in the public domain. Trademarks are considerably more expensive than copyrights, but the cost is worth it if you have a valuable asset and identifier to protect.

TM

- **Patents:** Patents are intended for inventions and are granted by the government to give you exclusive rights to make, use, and distribute your invention. Inventions refer to anything that is new or improves on an existing product or process. Your patent applies to your creation for twenty years in Canada from the date that you file your application for it.

- **Industrial designs:** According to the government: "An industrial design is the visual features of shape, configuration, pattern or ornament, or any combination of these features, applied to a finished article. For example, the shape of a table or the shape and decoration of a spoon may be industrial designs." You must create an original design to be eligible for this kind of protection. It gives you ten years of protection, though you may license or sell your design to others.

- **Trade secrets:** These are not formally protected by specific Canadian regulation and application, but a trade secret can have great value to a company. The often-cited secret recipe for Coca-Cola is one example. Keeping certain information secret ensures that it won't be copied or misused. They are usually protected by things like nondisclosure agreements, confidentiality clauses, software encryption, and even the good old-fashioned method of locking them away in a safe! In theory, these never expire, but it's the business's job to protect them.

"I am the inferior of any man whose rights I trample underfoot."

—HORACE GREELEY

OTHER LEGAL PROTECTIONS

There are probably several other areas where you'll need to consider the best ways to protect yourself against the unknown. What if someone finds a security fault in your software that allows them to break into others' accounts and steal private information? You might be liable for damages. Or, if you're opening a shop, you'll be in a public space, and you'll need comprehensive insurance to guard against just about anything unexpected, because people will invariably come up with creative ways to cause sticky legal situations. The usual things like fire and theft are obvious, but what if someone trips on something in your store and suffers an injury? Can they take legal action against you? Possibly. You need to make sure that you have all the appropriate protections in place. Here are some things to consider, as if you didn't have enough to worry about already!

- **Property insurance:** If your business is location-based, you'll need to investigate the kind of property insurance you need. This can protect against everything from fire and natural disasters to vandalism and theft. If you are renting, your agreement may include some terms of insurance, but this is by no means always the case. Many landlords expect their tenants to take out their own insurance policies.

- **Liability insurance:** Liability insurance is another protection you will need to consider, whether or not you have a physical location for your business. It protects against on-the-job physical injury, property damage (unless you have that covered elsewhere), lawsuits if someone is injured by your product or service, and lawsuits for slander, libel, claims of fraud or misleading advertising, etc. CYA, because someone out there may cause you trouble at some point!

- **Canada's anti-spam legislation (CASL):** There are strict laws in place about how you can market your company online. Hint: just sending out random emails to people who haven't signed up on your list is not one of them! For further information, see the Canadian government website. The link can be found in the Online Resources section of Resources at the back of the book.

- **Fraud awareness:** There are an endless number of scams out there, with scammers just waiting to separate you from your money in new and devious ways. You'll never be able to get familiar with them all, but there are some common techniques that are used over and over with gullible or less-than-vigilant businesses.

RAISING MONEY FOR YOUR BUSINESS: FIVE OPTIONS

Depending on the nature of your new business, you may need either very little money up-front or a sizable amount. It's certain that you'll need at least some, but only you can assess what your initial costs will be. There are a number of options out there for raising the money that you need, each with its advantages and drawbacks.

1. **Self-financing:** Your business may be quite small, a one-person operation with little overhead. Maybe you're setting yourself up as a life coach, or a computer repair person who does in-home visits. These kinds of professions don't usually require office space or a lot of equipment beyond the computer you already have. You may be able to start working on day one with almost no major investment. But you will still need to think about advertising and marketing, and what those will cost you. You might need to hire someone to do a new website if you don't feel confident in doing it yourself, though again, it's getting easier by the day to create professional-looking sites on your own. These days, it's entirely possible to start a business that can become profitable quickly with very little up-front payment on your part.

2. **Business loans:** A loan could be your best source of funding at the start. The only problem, of course, is that you have to pay it back! Also, how much you qualify for will depend very much on your own financial solvency (especially if you are a sole proprietor). Be sure to review how much you

need versus how much you'll be able to pay back monthly. You may want to start small to keep it more manageable.

3. **Venture capital:** VC funding is a complex topic, beyond the space a book like this permits, and honestly, it's probably beyond you right at the start. Most VC funders won't work with any business that hasn't already shown considerable promise and even profit. While the money they give out can be considerable (in the millions), you probably won't be looking at this option for a year or two or more, not until you can show what you've done so far and that you've grown your business in a significant way.

4. **Crowdfunding:** A relative newcomer to the field of fundraising, sites like Kickstarter and GoFundMe have become huge resources as a way to raise money for businesses and projects. Many have been successful in securing large amounts of money quickly, even exceeding expectations. This kind of funding works best when you are offering a product for sale, and just about anything you can imagine has been crowdfunded, from films to shoes, to games, to sports equipment. The only big drawback is that you have to deliver what you're promising, and on time, to the people who are funding you. You can get in trouble legally if you don't deliver things when you are supposed to do so. Making promises you can't keep will ruin your reputation quickly, and you'll be forced to give back whatever money you've raised. Different sites have different policies about how money is raised, with Kickstarter famously not giving you the money unless you raise all of it by a certain date, while other sites allow you to keep whatever you raised by that date, but they take a bigger cut as their fee. You'll have to research which option is right for you.

5. **Government grants for small businesses:** The Canadian government does offer some grants, but as you might imagine, they come with a lot of strings attached. Normally, you're expected to put up a portion of your total amount yourself, which can be anything from 10 percent all the way up to 50 percent. Sometimes, you have to be able to prove that your business will create new jobs, so if you're planning on going it alone, you won't qualify for many grants. Other grants are very specific to industry and territory. Different provinces also have their own specific grants, such as for students and young people, or for specific regions and industries. You'll have to do some research on your own province to see if there is anything that you may qualify for.

**"Ask thy purse
what thou should spend."**

—SCOTTISH PROVERB

TAXES (MORE UGH!)

Taxes are rarely on the list of most people's favorite subject, but as a small (and growing) business owner, you have no choice but to keep everything in order right from the start. You'll need to take the time to learn some basic tax law and practices, though ultimately you'll need to consult a professional to keep your money in order. The information and advice given here are not a substitute for help from a qualified accountant or other tax professional.

- **Learn about basic bookkeeping.** Though beyond the scope of this guide, learning about business income and expenses, and how to record them, will help you a great deal. If you already know someone who can do your bookkeeping for you, that's great, but even so, familiarize yourself with your incomings and outgoings, and keep an eye on your business's finances. The Further Reading section of Resources at the back of the book will offer you some great places to start.

- **Your tax return depends on the type of business.** If you are a small business that is a sole proprietorship or a simple partnership, you can report your business income on your T1, the personal income tax form. The T1 will include the T2125 Statement of Business or Professional Activities, which is what you will use to report all business income. If you are incorporated, you will need to fill out the T2, the corporate income tax return. Since you are not, legally speaking, your business, it needs its own tax return. Yes, you'll be filing two returns from now on, but that's the price you pay to be protected from any bad circumstances happening in your business.

- **You'll probably need to register for GST/HST.** Unless your gross business income is under $30,000 for four consecutive quarters (and there are some exceptions even for this), you'll need to register for goods and services tax (GST) and harmonized sales tax (HST). It's usually a good idea to register for these taxes even if you're currently making less than the required amount, because you can make use of Input Tax Credits, and claim back the GST and HST you've paid for any purchases directly related to your business.

- **You may need to register for provincial sales tax.** Depending on your location, you might need to register with your province to collect provincial sales tax (PST). This is true for Alberta, British Columbia, Manitoba, and Saskatchewan. If you are in Quebec, you must register to collect the Quebec Sales Tax (QST).

- **Always use an accountant.** Seriously, hire a good accountant. Obviously, unless you already have a superior knowledge of Canadian tax law, it's going to be to your benefit to consult a qualified accountant who can take care of all of these things for you. Don't skimp on this; make sure you hire someone with a good reputation who knows the ins and outs, and can get you all the deductions you're entitled to. Making mistakes with income taxes is not something you want to deal with later on, and you can be subject to penalties, additional tax owed, and late fees, among other consequences, if you mess it up, even in ignorance. Don't take the chance; go to a qualified professional!

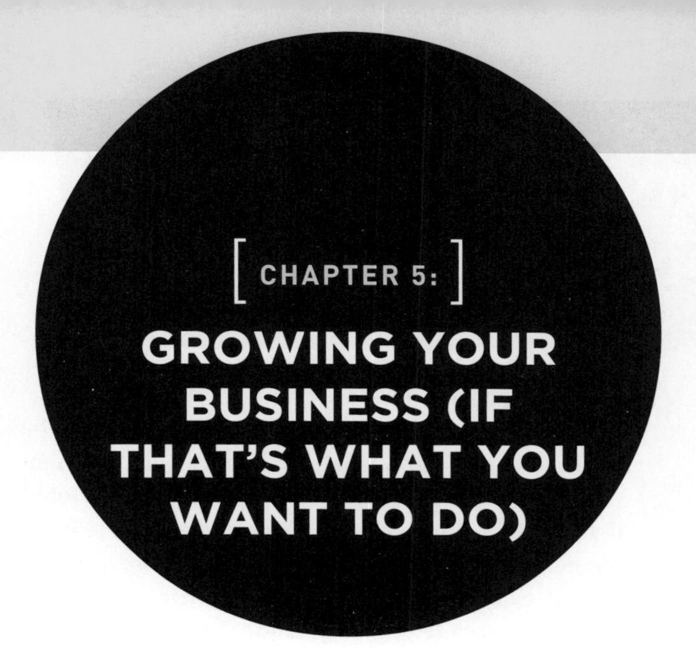

[CHAPTER 5:] GROWING YOUR BUSINESS (IF THAT'S WHAT YOU WANT TO DO)

At some point, your business will reach a stage where you may need to decide how you'll take the next step. Do you want to remain in the same place, or do you want to expand? The decision may be forced on you, if you have a growing customer/client base and not enough resources to satisfy demand. This is both exciting and potentially stressful. You'll need to make decisions about hiring or partnering with additional people, incorporating (if you're a sole proprietor), additional legal and financial requirements, and so on. How will you know what to do? Should you do anything at all? This chapter will give you some guidance on what to do when you may no longer be able to handle everything on your own, or when your partnership needs additional input and help.

ASSESSING WHAT YOU WANT YOUR BUSINESS TO BE AND DO: SEVEN THINGS TO CONSIDER

If you've had your business going for six months, a year, or more, you've no doubt already done check-ins to see where you are, what's been accomplished, and what the next step is. You *have* been doing this, right? If you're looking to grow your business and take it to the next step, there are any number of things you'll need to evaluate, from finances to growth potential, to sales figures to your reputation. Here are some important items to check in on.

1. **Your financial health:** One of the most important subjects for review, you need to examine your financial situation in depth. Look at your income statement (a document showing income, profit, and loss), a balance sheet (showing what you owe and what assets you possess), and a cash-flow statement (showing the liquidity of your money). Work with a good accountant and keep these documents in order, because they'll tell you a lot about how you're doing.

2. **Your customer/client satisfaction:** Assuming you have customers and/or clients, how happy are they with your services? How many do you actually have? Are you getting repeat customers? Is most

of your revenue coming from one or only a few clients? It shouldn't be. Are your clients recommending you to others? If so, are you seeing an increase in sales and business? This is what you want, of course, and if it's happening, it's a good sign.

3. **How you've grown so far:** How has your business grown over the past few months or year? Are you finding that you need to bring on an employee or two? Do you need more funding to take things to the next level? What do your partners think? Look back over the last twelve months especially and see where you are now versus a year ago. If the trajectory is upward, you're in good shape and ready to grow more.

4. **How close to your original business plan you are:** What about your plan has changed? What has stayed more or less the same? If you've found that you've gone back and had to revise your original plan, that's fine; it means that you're adapting to changes and could potentially mean that you have what it takes to survive in an ever-changing business environment. If your business is substantially different than how you first imagined it, is that for better or worse?

5. **What your industry is doing:** How is the overall industry? Is it thriving or hitting a slump? If things are going well, then it may be time for you to grow with it, to keep up with new demands. If it's slowing down, what can you do to keep yourself going through the tougher times ahead? Can you still expand, or do you need to put the brakes on that idea for a while?

6. **What your competitors are doing:** How is your competition faring? Are they growing and expanding? If so, you might need to do the same to keep up. Healthy competition is also a sign of a healthy industry, which means that there's room for more than one business offering similar

services. If you're doing better than they are, that's awesome! If they're doing better than you, well then, you have your work cut out for you!

7. **What your reputation is:** What do people think of your business, six months or a year in? Are you making a splash? Is it a good splash? Or are you still wallowing in obscurity, waiting for your moment? If you have a loyal customer/client base who is spreading the word about you, you're in a good position.

> **"Some days you're smiling and thinking you're going to make this thing rock. Then the next day a pipe breaks and your costs look too high. You have to learn to keep your eyes on an ultimate goal. If you lose sight of that goal, you have to get out."**
>
> ***—HAMDI ULUKAYA (FOUNDER AND CEO OF CHOBANI)***

DO YOU NEED TO EXPAND? EIGHT SIGNS THAT YOU SHOULD

Then first question to ask yourself is simple: Is expansion necessary? The answer may not be entirely up to you. You may be comfortable with the way your business is going and not want to rock the boat or take additional risks just yet, but there could be external pressures that might force you into expanding. Whether you want to do it or not, here are some key signs that you might need to consider growing your business and taking it to the next level.

1. **You have more customers or clients than you can handle.** This is every small business's dream, and a goal that you strive for, but it can bring with it a whole new set of problems. Maybe you, as a sole proprietor in sales, can't fill orders fast enough. Maybe you have too many people wanting to be your clients, and not enough time to give them each the attention they deserve. For whatever reasons, you may have no choice but to seek out help.

2. **Your customers or clients consistently want more from you.** Along with too many people wanting what you offer, maybe they also want *more* of what you offer. If you run a yoga studio, maybe people are requesting Pilates or Tai Chi, but you don't have a certification to teach those; it may be time to hire someone who does. Or maybe your online mail-order company sells great clothing, but people keep asking for

something you don't make or don't have the skill to make; you may need to hire on someone who can. When your customers or clients tell you that they want more, listen!

3. **You've outgrown your space.** If you have a physical space, whether a shop or an office, maybe it's just not working for you anymore. You may be stocking too much merchandise, or perhaps your shop isn't in an ideal location anymore.

4. **You don't have the necessary skills to do something.** Maybe you've been able to coast along as a sole proprietor for a while, but suddenly your taxes or legal situation are getting more complex and you can't handle them on your own. Maybe your website needs a massive overhaul and someone who can maintain it, and you either don't have the time or the ability to take care of everything. Maybe you're a partnership, but you all decide that you need a new specialist to come in to take care of certain projects, someone with more expertise than any of you have. This is a clear sign that you'll need to do some hiring.

5. **You've discovered the perfect product or service.** Maybe it's less an issue of demand (though that can be there, too), but that you've finally found the exact product or service you've been trying to perfect, and the customer response has been fantastic. Sometimes, just having a hunch that things are going to get bigger is something you need to pay attention to. Be careful not to just talk yourself into something, but if your product or service is getting rave reviews and feedback, it's a pretty clear sign that there might be a much bigger demand for it fairly soon. Consider what you'll need to do to grow to meet that demand.

6. **You're relying too much on one source of income.** This is actually a negative. If you have one client that's giving you a substantial amount of money, that's great, but be careful about relying on that. It's great while it lasts, but circumstances change. Maybe their business or financial situation will take a turn for the worse, and instead of giving you 35 percent of your revenue, they're now only giving you 10 percent. This can cause huge problems. It's the old adage about not having all your eggs in one basket. If you have one awesome client, you need to grow and find more, to make sure that you're not counting on that income.

7. **You're consistently profitable.** If you're always in the black, that's a very good sign that you're doing the right things, and can be a good indication that you need to consider expanding. If you're not in debt and not losing money, look at ways you can take some of that extra cash and put it into expansion, even if only in small areas at first. You don't want to squander your good fortune, but just sitting on extra money that could be working for you is a waste as well.

8. **Your industry is expanding.** Keep tabs on what your field is up to. If it's growing, then it's likely that you'll need to grow with it. If the thing you offer is all the rage right now, take advantage of that and look at ways that you can grow your business to meet the new demand. These cycles never last forever, of course, but if you can ride the wave while the market is hot, you can do very well.

HOW TO EXPAND: NINE IDEAS

So you know that it's time to start growing, but what should you do next? You'll have many options, based on your type of business, but there are some basic steps you should consider, regardless of your industry and focus. Use these ideas and adapt them to your personal situation.

1. **Cultivate your existing market(s).** The best place to start is with your existing clients and customers. These are the ones who already know you and are more open to your new offerings. Turning existing customers into loyal repeat customers is easier than reaching out cold to new people who may know nothing about you. Do some more in-depth analysis on your current markets, sometimes called a market segmentation analysis. This will allow you to break these markets into specific groups and demographics: age, location, buying history, etc. This in turn will allow you to focus your new products and services on exactly where they need to go.

2. **Add new products and services, but gradually.** You probably already have in mind the kind of add-ons you'd like to introduce. If you have a loyal target market, they will be eager for more! Look at creating products and services that you can cross-sell (i.e., that complement what you already have). How will you know what people want? One of the simplest ways to do this is just to ask them. Create a survey or questionnaire, and offer a small gift or bonus in return for their honest answers. If you have some new offerings in mind, run them

past some test groups and see which ones have the most appeal. But be careful about flooding them with too many new choices all at once. Studies repeatedly show that when people are given too many options, they most often end up choosing none of them. Give each new offering you have time to grow and space to breathe, so that each gets the attention it deserves.

3. **Work on widening your sales funnel.** The sales funnel is a model that can be thought of like a real funnel: wide at the top and narrow at the bottom. This is a good analogy for your process of attracting customers and clients. There will be many people out there (the wide portion of the funnel), but more and more will leave off and not go the whole distance (the narrow end of the funnel). Each person goes through a series of phases: awareness, being interested, evaluating what you offer, making a decision, and then purchasing. At each phase, the funnel gets narrower as fewer and fewer people are interested in making the decision to buy. If you have a healthy portion of people at the narrow end, then it's worth making the effort to widen the funnel by working to attract more initial interest.

4. **Hire new people.** It may be that you'll have to bring on new staff. If you're a sole proprietor, this might feel strange, especially if you've done everything yourself up until now. If you're in a partnership, you may be looking for an additional partner (or more), or also deciding that you need to take on some employees to handle the day-to-day activities that you no longer have time for. The sections that follow in this chapter go into much more detail about the process of deciding whom you need, how to find them, and whom to hire.

5. **Look for new target markets.** This is perhaps the most obvious choice when you're trying to grow, but it's also a lot easier said than done! You'll need to go back to the drawing board with your original business

plan and conduct new market research to see what new target markets might be reachable with your additional offerings. This will take time and work, and may be frustrating and even boring, but it's going to be essential if you want to bring in new customers. One way to help start the flow is to offer your existing customers and clients some kind of freebie or bonus if they bring you new business. Word of mouth still carries a lot of weight, and the more your existing base can recommend you, the better!

6. **Consider your existing reach.** Is yours a local business only, or does it have customers across your province or even the whole country? If you're a small brick-and-mortar shop, you may not be able to do much expansion, unless you're opening a second location, but if you have an online presence for sales and clientele, it's well worth expanding your reach as far as you reasonably can. You may be limited to Canada at the moment, but perhaps the United States and overseas markets are possibilities. You'll need to consider what it is that makes your offering valuable, and why people in a new location would want it.

7. **Look at strategic partnerships.** Are there other businesses that you can partner with on a project or a promotion? What about a charity or nonprofit? The idea is to work together toward a common goal (i.e., getting both of you more attention) that benefits you both. Sponsoring a benefit for a charity can be a great way to give yourself visibility and give something back to the community. It will cost you money to do, but the free advertising and goodwill will pay for themselves. In the case of proposing a business partnership, try to see if there is a business that needs what you do, and/or vice versa. Look for ways that you could collaborate together and make use of each other's markets. It might just be a joint advertising campaign, or you might actually design a product or service together.

8. **Consider trade shows.** Depending on your business, there may be a trade show or conference devoted to your industry; in fact, there are

probably a lot of them! These can be a great way to get you in front of more people and advertise your wares and services. They offer chances to network and connect with new and influential people that might open new doors. Trade shows aren't free, though, and some exhibitors put large amounts of money into renting prime space, having elaborate booths, and so on. So be mindful of your budget before going this route, and only take on what you can actually afford.

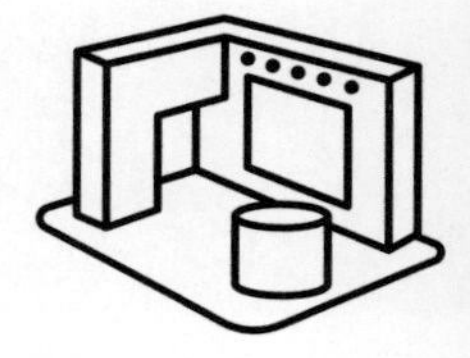

9. **Keep an eye on your competition.** What are your competitors doing? Are they ahead of you or behind you? What can you learn from their methods that could help you? Research their ad campaigns and marketing strategies to see what makes them tick. Did they try something that was wildly successful? Would a similar approach work for you, or would you just be seen as copying them? What ways of marketing and advertising are they not doing that you might be able to capitalize on? You always need to consider the actions of others and the position of the larger industry you're in.

WHAT ABOUT LICENSING? FIVE TIPS

Licensing can be a very good way to grow your business and bring in substantial amounts of money. Basically, a company can "rent" its intellectual property to another business, which then uses that brand for their own content and pays a fee back to the company. A T-shirt company that licenses famous cartoon characters to appear on their shirts is a simple example. Think about Disney for a good example of getting one's characters and property on all sorts of everyday items. In any licensing transaction there are two parties, the licensor who owns the brand and licensee who wants to rent it. As a smaller business, you might not have anything that you can offer up to others to license, but you might be able to add the brand of a bigger, more famous company to your own products or services. Here are some tips when looking to license another company's property.

1. **Seek out a company that has proven value.** If you're going to try to get a license, seek out companies that are in line with your mission and your values. There needs to be some kind of logical connection between the two offerings. If you own a fitness center, offering to license athletic clothing or shoes in your advertising and sell them on-

site is a good example. Make sure it's something you believe in and want your own customers and clients to share in. Don't try to sell something just because it's a bigger company and they agreed to take you on as a partner. You'll have a longer partnership if you're in accord with each other.

2. **Be worthy of their attention.** Bigger companies are naturally quite wary of keeping their reputations in a good light, and if you are approaching them about using something of theirs, they're going to want to make sure that you are worth their time and their money. You have to have a proven track record and show that you are successful enough to produce something with their brand. Think about it: Would you rent out your brilliant idea to everyone that asked? Of course not! You'd want to prove that they could deliver and not tarnish your brand and reputation. So, be worthy of their trust.

3. **Understand what their guidelines and restrictions will be.** It will be absolutely crucial for you to understand how you can use this brand and, more important, how you *can't* use it. Companies are very protective of their hard-won brand reputations, and you will probably be granted very limited use. If you make clothing, you may only be able to use the brand on specific items. If you overstep and put it on your other clothing lines, you'll be in big trouble. You may be limited as to where and when you can sell the item. The reverse of this is that most companies don't limit themselves regarding whom they license to. You may be able to put a specific brand on your shoes, for example, and the licensing company will expect you to produce those shoes with their brand on them, at least in Canada. But there's nothing to prevent them creating a license for a similar shoe made by another small business and only sold in India, for example. They will probably retain that right, and there's nothing you can do about it. The company will also have quality assurance requirements, to make sure that you're not turning out something cheap

and junky with their name on it. Basically, you'll need to go along with whatever terms they offer.

4. **Understand the royalty rate.** The royalty is what you will pay out of your sales back to the company for the right to use their brand. There is no set rate in a legal sense, but most bigger companies probably do have their own policies about what they'll charge. And these will probably be pretty inflexible, unless they really see an opportunity. Often you'll also have to pay a flat rate up-front, so make sure that your budget can accommodate what they're asking. If it's a brand you really want, you'll pretty much have to grin and bear it, and give them what they want.

5. **Seek out professional help.** Obviously, this can all get tremendously complicated very quickly. Don't even think about going it alone. Seek out help in the form of a licensing agent or attorney that specializes in such things. You want to make sure that everything is covered and there are no misunderstandings in the licensing contract. Any mistakes will likely be seen as your fault, and could damage your own business significantly. If you blow a licensing agreement with a big company, your reputation will be tarnished, and that may keep you from ever licensing anything again. Do it right the first time.

DO YOU NEED EMPLOYEES? SEVEN SIGNS THAT YOU DO

If you find yourself at the stage of maybe needing to expand, one of the key questions you'll have to ask yourself is: Do you need to hire someone, or, if you already have employees, do you need to hire someone else? This will largely depend on your business, its profitability, and how it's grown so far. You'll have to look at a number of factors beyond just the financial to see if it's feasible, or even desirable. Here are some of the main signs that it's time to think about bringing someone else on board.

1. **You need certain skills that no one else does at the moment.** This is probably the most obvious sign. You have need of a set of skills that you or your partners (if you have them) don't possess. If you're finding that a specialist is required and it's not someone you can hire as a freelancer (it will be an ongoing job), then you need to consider bringing someone on permanently. Not having those skills in your arsenal is only going to hurt your business growth in the long run.

2. **You're wasting valuable time on other work.** If you have to take time out of your own duties and responsibilities to take care of tasks that are important, but not what you need to be focusing on, then you definitely need to hire someone to do them for you. This can include things like administrative work, website maintenance, and marketing and

selling. These are all essential, but they may not be the things you need to be doing. When you first started out, maybe you could wear every hat, but it's likely that at some point, some of those jobs are going to have to be delegated.

3. **You're having trouble keeping up with client or customer needs.** If you are not able to manage the needs of your customers or clients, this is bad. You may even be in danger of losing them, which is worse. You may be missing deadlines, or not returning vital phone calls, or not shipping products when you promised them, all of which will anger your base and make you look unreliable, which is the last thing you want. Alternately, you may be able to handle the existing workload, but you may not be able to take on any new clients, and you may find yourself turning down valuable new ones, or being unable to fulfill an order from a big company or client, all of which will lose you money and keep you from growing as fast as you should be doing. These are definite signs that someone (or several someones) needs to come aboard and help out.

4. **You know the job description that you need.** If you can already write out the exact job description of the person you need for the job, then you *need* that person. It's really that simple. It means that you've already got it worked out in your mind just what they'll need to do. Whether it's a part-time job or a full forty-hour week, if you have enough to keep someone busy, then that person should be working for you. It probably means that you're currently doing work that's taking time away from other things (see above), and you can create an entire position of work that you don't have time for.

5. **You're feeling overworked.** If you're taking work home or working late into the night (if you already work from home), then you're damaging your work/life balance and are in need of some relief. At first,

you may feel like you need to be in charge of everything, and you'll be prepared to work fourteen-hour days to make sure it all happens. Yet this will not only get old over time, but also it will affect your health and your ability to even do your job. Seriously, don't work yourself into the ground, no matter what some entrepreneurs tell you. You're not going to help yourself by ruining your physical and/or mental health. If you want your business to last, you need to pace yourself and keep some perspective. Your business is important, but it can't be the only thing you do.

6. **It will bring in more money.** This is kind of a no-brainer. If bringing someone new in will help bring in more money, more customers, more clients, more everything, then yes, you definitely need to hire someone! Maybe you need an ace salesperson or marketer who can take the business to the next level. If they can do this, then it will be more than worth the cost to bring them on board and let them work their magic. Your outlay at the beginning will pay off many times over.

7. **Your financial situation can handle it.** Obviously, this is going to be one of your biggest concerns. You may need all kinds of specialist help, but if you don't have the budget for it, there's not much you can do, except wait until you do. That can be very frustrating, so you'll need to focus on doing everything you can to get yourself in the position to bring in new hires. Whether that involves increasing sales or something else, such as seeking out external funding, will depend on your situation. Be very careful about hiring anyone until you know you can afford it. You never want to be in the situation of having to let someone go because you can no longer afford them. Bear in mind that the new hire will also have to get up to speed with your business, and that may require a bit of extra training from you or one of your partners. Do you have the time to spare to do that? You'll need to.

SEVEN WAYS TO LOCATE THE RIGHT PEOPLE

If you've made the decision to bring one or more people into your business, congratulations! It's a big next step and will see you along the way to further success. But before you do it, you have to get clear in your mind about whom you need and how you're going to go about it. The days of just placing an ad in the local paper are long gone (though maybe that still works sometimes?). There are a number of options for seeking out potential employees, and some are better than others. Here are some tips for making sure that you don't waste your time on pointless attempts and instead can locate the people you need quickly.

1. **Advertise locally.** We joke about advertising in the paper, but you know what? There are far worse ways to get the word out than using your local media. Bringing in someone who's already local offers many advantages, since they'll know the area and may already be settled. This is not to say that you can't look farther afield, but consider that the person you need might be in your own proverbial backyard. Local media can get the word out to the talent that's in the area.

2. **Make good use of LinkedIn.** Since LinkedIn is so focused on networking and on people looking to hire and be hired, it should be one

of your first ports of call. If you are member of any LinkedIn groups, you might be able to post about what you're looking for in them, though be sure that this is acceptable first. There may be groups for posting job listings in your area or industry, so seek those out and let people come to you. It's also fine to search for people on the site and see who comes up. Maybe you'll find some potential candidates who might be a great fit. If so, you can reach out to them directly. You should already be doing this, even if you don't have a job to offer right away. The more you build relationships, the better you'll do when the hiring search begins in earnest.

3. **Consider using other social media sites.** Facebook and Twitter can also be useful if you have pages there with good solid followings. Again, you never know who's following you. A short notice on Twitter with a link to the job description on your website might yield some good results. And Facebook still has an enormous number of users, despite its recent problems and security concerns. You have the freedom to offer a full description there (unlike Twitter), or link back to your site. The advantage of both these sites, of course, is the option to share your post (and encourage your followers to do it!), which helps spread the message even father.

4. **Take advantage of your network and word of mouth.** If you've spent time networking (and you should!), you'll have any number of professional contacts. This is the ideal time to check in with them and let them know what you're doing. And as networking is a give-and-take situation, be clear that you'll happily return the favor if any of your contacts need assistance in finding their own perfect hires. The more you can help each other out, the better everyone will be. If you've already got a good reputation (and you should!), it's very possible that someone in your network will be willing to give you a helping hand and refer some potential candidates to you.

5. **Look into advertising in trade publications.** What business publications do you read, whether online or in print? There are probably

some devoted to your industry, so consider advertising your job with them. These periodicals are being read by hundreds, if not thousands, of other professionals on a regular basis, and you'll be fairly confident of having narrowed down your search if you know that people from your industry are seeking you out after seeing your job listing.

6. **Ask your clients.** If you have satisfied customers and users, reach out to them and mention that you are expanding and hiring. You never know who's using your products and services that might jump at the chance to apply. This gives you a head start, because they will already be familiar with you, and presumably at least something of a fan. Why not bring in an enthusiastic client to help you out? It could be a win-win for both sides! If you have a mailing list, let the recipients know about your plans in one of your regular posts. Also, post it to your company blog (you *do* have one, right?). If you like, consider offering a finder's fee or some kind of prize if someone refers you to a person that you end up hiring. It's an incentive for people to give you a helping hand.

7. **Consider a recruiter.** They can be expensive, they take a cut of your money, and they may not be your first choice, but there are advantages to using them, if your company is at a stage where you can afford it and the benefits are worth it. They'll do the work of finding great candidates for you, they have internal networks and loads of hiring experience, they'll save you all the time so you can focus on your business (instead of endless rounds of advertising), and they can probably find suitable candidates much faster than you can, since that's their main job. They'll also be better at recognizing suitable fits for your job description, and will probably be able to sell your position better than you can. They're not the choice (or an option) for everyone, and if your business is still small, it's an option that's probably out of your budget range. But if you try one and it works out, you may end up developing a good relationship that can carry forward with future hires. That way you'll always know that you're getting the best people, which will be money well spent!

NINE TIPS WHEN INTERVIEWING AND HIRING

The process of interviewing and hiring potential candidates can be exhausting and fraught with peril. You're making a big decision to bring someone else on board, and it could work out amazingly or it could fail completely. No pressure, though! Depending on whether you're hiring just one person or several, there are ways to vet candidates that will save you time and a lot of stress. Here is a guide to the kinds of interview questions and preparations you should make.

1. **Be on time.** Nothing presents more unprofessionally than being late, especially at a first meeting. Never do this. Give your candidate the respect of honoring their time and be there early.

2. **Be prepared.** As with punctuality, you need to have everything ready: their resume/CV, any references they've provided, your own background research, a list of the topics you'll cover and the questions you'll ask, etc. You may have been lucky enough to attract some very qualified individuals who see promise in your business and are willing to work for you instead of someone else. Don't prove them wrong by being sloppy or disorganized. Make the effort to present yourself at your very best, because in some ways they're interviewing you, too.

3. **Be friendly and put them at ease.** Interviewing can be a stressful process for both parties, but probably more so for the candidate. Dispel any tension by being friendly and welcoming. Make a bit of small talk at the beginning to get the conversation going. If you have anything in common (as seen on their resume), bring it up as a conversation starter. The idea is to get you both more relaxed and comfortable so that you can both be at your best.

4. **Watch how they conduct themselves.** How they behave will be very telling. It may seem a bit unfair, but these first impressions can actually say a lot about the person. How are they dressed? They may not need to wear formal business attire, but if their clothing is wrinkled, unwashed, not even remotely businesslike, it may be at least a yellow flag. Again, this may not matter if your primary office is your living room. How do they act? Do they put their feet up on the table or act extremely casually? None of these actions should necessarily be disqualifying, but they might be early warning signs that the person may not take the job as seriously as you'd like. If a candidate is not interested in impressing you, what does that say about them?

5. **Ask the right questions.** Make a comprehensive list of questions that you want to ask ahead of time. Practice reading them out. You know what you're looking for, so make sure you cover all the points that are important to you. Other questions will probably come up spontaneously during the course of the interview, and it's possible you may not get to ask everything that you wanted to, but try to cover all the most important ones. Make your list in order of importance, from the things that you really must know down to the questions that might be more for your own interest. One of the best ways to gauge their ability is to set them a situation or problem (maybe something you've already encountered), and ask how they would go about solving it. This will give you some insights into their working mind and how they might perform on the job.

6. **Answer all questions to the best of your ability.** Your candidate will likely have a list of their own questions for you, so be prepared to go into as much detail as you need to answer them. If you don't know the answer to something, don't bluff. Say so honestly, and commit to finding out the answer and getting back to them. Then, actually go find the answer and get back to them! You need to be able to show that you take their questions and concerns seriously. All of this relies on your knowing your business better than anyone, which you already do, right?

7. **Be very mindful that certain questions are not permitted.** You may be interested in the candidate's personal life, or information that's not on their resume, to get a better sense of who they are and how they might fit in. This is fine, but be very aware that there are many kinds of questions that you cannot ask during an interview. These are governed by provincial and even federal laws, so you need to familiarize yourself with any restrictions. You don't want to give the appearance of engaging in job discrimination; this could result in legal troubles and a bad reputation. You are *not* permitted to ask questions about any of the following: age, ethnicity, national origin, First Nations status, gender identity, sexual orientation, religion or lack thereof, marital status, if the candidate is pregnant or considering it, personal finances, political affiliation . . . you get the idea! The point is that the candidate is there to be considered on their merits, not on anything about themselves. If they volunteer information that could stray into one of these categories, it's best to either ignore it, or suggest sticking to the main topic (i.e., the job). You never want to give the impression that you are considering anything other than their qualifications for the job.

8. **Make your decision.** This is the most difficult part, because you may have more than one suitable candidate for the job (if you're lucky!). You'll need to consider their qualifications and references, the opinions of your partners (if you have any), and your own judgment. Generally, you

want to be looking for someone who is enthusiastic, asks questions, is open to change and growth, works well with others, and has the skills you need but without an attitude. Yes, this is a wish list, and you may not find the perfect match, but you may just find someone close enough. If the person would be a good fit overall and can do the jobs you need them to do, then you have a likely hire.

9. **Follow up with all candidates.** You have an obligation to let those you didn't hire know. Do it as soon as you can; it's rude to keep people waiting. Send each candidate a personalized email letting them know that you went with someone else. You don't need to go into details about why you made your choice or didn't hire them. In fact, it's better if you don't, as anything you say could be used by a disgruntled rejected person as evidence of discrimination. You've made your decision, so thank them for their time, and leave it at that.

"The employer generally gets the employees he deserves."

—SIR WALTER BILBEY

LEGAL AND FINANCIAL INFORMATION ABOUT EMPLOYEES

When you finally make your decision about whom to hire, you'll have certain legal and financial obligations. Laws vary according to each province, but here is a short list of things that you'll have to acquire or report.

- **Social Insurance Number (SIN).** As you are no doubt aware, all employees need to have this number, and almost all will, so it shouldn't be a problem. But a potential employee *must* have this number to work legally in Canada, so don't ignore it.

- **If a potential hire is not a Canadian citizen:** If you've found the perfect candidate, but they are not a citizen, you can still hire them provided they present an original copy of one of the following documents, which allow them to apply for an SIN at a Service Canada, if they haven't already:

  - **A Permanent Resident Card**
  - **A Confirmation of Permanent Residence**
  - **A Record of Landing**
  - **A Verification of Landing**
  - **A Verification of Status**

- **Obtaining the SIN.** As an employer, you must have the individual's SIN within three days of them starting to work for you. According to the Canadian government's website on SINs: "Employers must be informed of each new employee's SIN within three (3) days after the day on which their employment begins, and maintain a record of the SIN of the employee so they can provide him or her with Records of Employment and various year-end reporting slips such as the T4 for income tax purposes. Employers also use SINs to record and forward employee payroll deductions for income tax, the Employment Insurance (EI) program, Canada Pension Plan (CPP) or Québec Pension Plan (QPP), and Quebec Parental Insurance Plan (QPIP)."

- **Tax forms.** Employees will need to fill out the TD1 form (Personal Tax Credit Return), both the federal form and one for the province where they live and will be working. These forms are used to determine how much tax you need to deduct from their pay. If your business is based in Quebec, the employee will need to fill out the TD1 for the federal and Form TP1015.3-V (Source Deductions Return) for the province. If you have any questions, refer to the government tax sites in the Resources section at the end of the book.

- **A job contract.** This is not absolutely necessary, but most advisers recommend that you have a legal agreement drawn up that defines the job and its responsibilities. You should also include salary, hours, any perks the employee receives, etc. This is a good way to clarify everything at the start and not let any confusion creep in later on. It also binds the employee to any terms that you set down. Your employee should sign, and you or a representative (or partner) should sign and provide the employee with a copy, while keeping one on file yourself.

- **Nondisclosure agreements.** If you are working on anything that is proprietary, it's necessary to have any employees sign this kind of agreement. This doesn't have to be about top-secret information or sensitive material; it can also mean that you don't want an employee discussing software design or plans for a new product line until the launch. It's a way of protecting your business from less-ethical competitors who might be very interested in what you're up to. Your type of business may not need one of these, but if you decide that you do, remember that they are very serious and not to be taken lightly. If an employee breaks the agreement, you need to be able to take appropriate legal action. Have your lawyer draw up any needed documents so that you get the wording right.

"The only thing that hurts more than paying an income tax is not having to pay an income tax."

—THOMAS R. DEWAR

TEN STRATEGIES FOR KEEPING YOUR BUSINESS ON TRACK FOR GROWTH

If you've made it this far, congratulations! Your business is growing, and, over time, even thriving. You may have reached several plateaus along the way and can look back with pride over what you've accomplished so far. But there's a still a lot to do! There will always be more room for growth, and the potential for additional employees, new products and services, and more. What can you do to keep your business on track to continue your success? Here are some tips.

1. **Use the internet wisely.** No matter what kind of business you have, you can't afford not to be online. This should be obvious by now, but not every small business makes use of the internet the way it could and should. Keep your website looking professional and always have it up-to-date, cultivate an email newsletter, have a blog, advertise strategically, get your SEO in order . . . all of these things will help to keep you visible in the most important potential market there is.

2. **Keep an eye on the competition.** It's essential that you watch what your competitors (friendly or otherwise) do. This doesn't mean engaging in corporate espionage or doing anything illegal; it just means keeping tabs on what they're up to. Read blogs, look at new product

launches and new services, track their growth, whom they're hiring, where they are and if they're relocating, etc. It also doesn't mean that you need to try to keep up, but if you know what competitors are doing relative to your own situation, you'll be in a better place to make your own decisions about your next moves.

3. **Be thinking about the long term.** If you've made it to a year, that's great! Now, what are your plans for the next year? For five years from now? If you've shown yourself and the world that your business might just be around a while, you need to be thinking about that "while" very seriously. You should have been doing that from the start, of course, but now is the time to get more focused. Where do you see your business going? What would you like to do? Will you stick with it or pass it on to someone else? You need to be constantly asking yourself the bigger questions!

4. **Cultivate your existing customers or clients.** Never forget who got you this far. You should always think of ways of thanking and rewarding your existing base, while continuing to cultivate them as repeat customers and clients, the type that will be loyal in the long run and will recommend you to others. Incentives, discounts, loyalty programs, and referral fees are just some ways you can appeal to them. Look for ways to show your appreciation and keep them around.

5. **Hire as you need, and do so strategically.** Follow the guidelines for hiring and bring in the people you need, when you need them, and when you can afford them. If you're a small business, be careful about whom you take on board; you literally can't afford to bring in the wrong people. It will pay off to wait until you have a match that you think will really work. Decide on exactly the jobs you need and fill those positions. Don't hire just for the sake of it, or because you have some extra money.

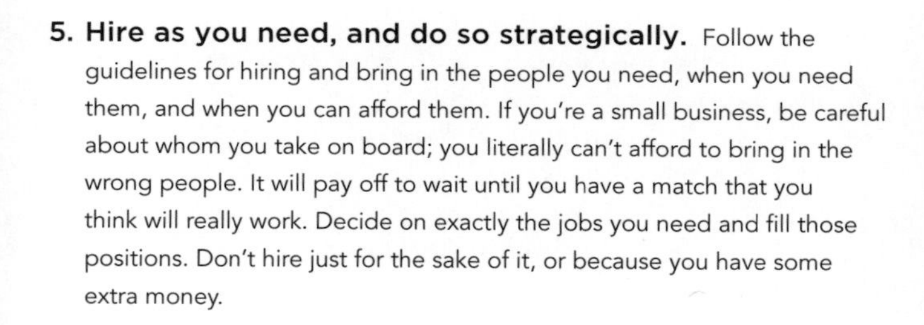

6. **Manage your time wisely.** Keeping on top of your time may seem impossible, but it will be a tremendous help when the going gets tough (and it probably already has for you at this stage!). Learn how to prioritize your time and tasks to focus on the things that most need your attention, while delegating less important work to others, or at least saving it until later. A full discussion of time management is outside the bounds of this book. For much more information, see *This Book Will Teach You to Own Your Time*, also in this series.

7. **Review your company and yourself on a regular basis.** You need to check in with your business regularly. How are you situated in the industry? How are you managing in the overall economy? Go back to your original business plan and look it over. Revise anything that has changed or needs to be changed. Some things may not be as relevant anymore, while others may have grown in importance. Review how you, your partners, and your employees are working. What are you doing well? What could be done better? Always be tweaking and refining.

8. **Understand and keep on top of your financial situation.** This is one of the most crucial pieces of advice you will receive. Your finances are essential to your survival, and you need to be very careful in managing them. You need an accurate accounting of everything, and it is worth your time and investment to get outside help with this, if you don't have someone who's a whiz with finances on your staff (and if you do, that's great!). You need someone who understands tax law, write-offs, exemptions, etc. If you have debt in the form of a business loan, you need to keep a close eye on it. You need to watch your overall budget and make sure that you can afford to employ the people you want to employ. Yes, all of this can be tedious and boring, but your business won't survive without it.

9. **Adapt as your business grows.** You need to be prepared for the unexpected to happen, both good and bad. Don't become rigid and inflexible. You may have to take an alternate path to a goal you were working on, and that can be just fine. Be open to change, and adapt as your business grows. There will be things you never saw coming, but if you can go with the flow, you'll have a better shot at surviving in the long run.

10. **Never forget who you are.** Amid all of this, you need to be careful not to lose yourself. Yes, in many ways, you are your business and it's a very important part of you, but it can't be the only thing that you do or focus on. Before you came up with this amazing idea, you were a person with other interests, and you need to make sure you check in with that person on a regular basis. Don't neglect your hobbies and interests, because they will keep you sane and give you a break to recharge your batteries. You'll be able to return to your work a little bit refreshed if you keep a healthy distance from it sometimes. And for goodness' sake, don't neglect your friends and family. If you have children, that time is precious and goes fast. Don't waste all of it throwing yourself into your work every day. It will still be there, but that short time won't be. Own your business; don't be a slave to it.

RESOURCES

This book is by necessity limited in the information it can contain, but there is a limitless amount of additional information out there to help you. This extensive bibliography will give you a lot to digest in the coming months as you plan your new business and prepare for success!

FURTHER READING

This list includes both general guides to entrepreneurship, and more specific guides to marketing, sales, bookkeeping, etc. While many are from U.S.-based authors, much of the information is still valid. See the Online Resources section below for Canadian-specific information. There is a wealth of information here that will keep you busy reading and learning for a long time.

Bill Aulet, *Disciplined Entrepreneurship: 24 Steps to a Successful Startup* (John Wiley, 2013).

Charles Bamford and Garry Bruton, *Entrepreneurship: The Art, Science, and Process for Success*, 3rd edition (McGraw-Hill Education, 2018).

Rajat Bhargava, *The Startup Playbook* (Lioncrest Publishing, 2018).

Jeb Blount, *Fanatical Prospecting: The Ultimate Guide to Opening Sales Conversations and Filling the Pipeline by Leveraging Social Selling, Telephone, Email, Text, and Cold Calling* (John Wiley, 2015).

Ken Colwell, *Starting a Business QuickStart Guide: The Simplified Beginner's Guide to Launching a Successful Small Business, Turning Your Vision into Reality, and Achieving Your Entrepreneurial Dream* (ClydeBank Media, 2019).

Alejandro Cremades, *The Art of Startup Fundraising: Pitching Investors, Negotiating the Deal, and Everything Else Entrepreneurs Need to Know* (John Wiley, 2016).

Allan Dib, *The 1-Page Marketing Plan: Get New Customers, Make More Money, and Stand Out from the Crowd* (Page Two, 2018).

Abraham Douglas, *Bookkeeping: Beginners Guide to Basic Bookkeeping and Accounting Principles to Build a Successful Business* (Independently published, 2019).

Jeffrey Gitomer, *The Sales Bible, New Edition: The Ultimate Sales Resource* (John Wiley, 2015).

Seth Godin, *This Is Marketing: You Can't Be Seen until You Learn to See* (Portfolio, 2018).

David Hoffeld, *The Science of Selling: Proven Strategies to Make Your Pitch, Influence Decisions, and Close the Deal* (Tarcher Perigee, 2016).

Anthony Iannarino, *The Only Sales Guide You'll Ever Need* (Penguin Random House, 2016).

Kevin D. Johnson, *The Entrepreneur Mind: 100 Essential Beliefs, Characteristics, and Habits of Elite Entrepreneurs* (Johnson Media, 2013).

Andrew Macarthy, *500 Social Media Marketing Tips: Essential Advice, Hints and Strategy for Business: Facebook, Twitter, Pinterest, Google+, YouTube, Instagram, LinkedIn, and More!* (Independently published, 2018).

Steve Mariotti, *The Young Entrepreneur's Guide to Starting & Running a Business* (Currency, 2014).

Heidi M. Neck, Christopher P. Neck, and Emma L. Murray, *Entrepreneurship: The Practice and Mindset* (SAGE Publications, 2017).

Adam Richards, *Sales: Mastering The Art of Selling: 10 Mistakes to Avoid Like the Plague, 12 Powerful Techniques to Reveal Any Hidden Objections & Close the Sale* (Independently published, 2016).

Mike Roberge, *The Sales Acceleration Formula: Using Data, Technology, and Inbound Selling to Go from $0 to $100 Million* (John Wiley, 2015).

David S. Rose, *The Startup Checklist: 25 Steps to a Scalable, High-Growth Business* (John Wiley, 2016).

Mike Weinberg, *Sales Truth: Debunk the Myths. Apply Powerful Principles. Win More New Sales* (Harper Collins Leadership, 2019).

ONLINE RESOURCES

The internet is a limitless source of information. This list gives you all sorts of valuable content about starting a business in Canada, as well as professional associations that may be of use to you. And it is by no means exhaustive. What good fortune that we have all of this (mostly) free information available to us now!

Adweek

A site by subscription filled with excellent articles on news, marketing, advertising, using digital tools and much more. If your business is at the right place and your budget allows for it, this might be worth your money.
adweek.com

Canadian Chamber of Commerce

From their website: "With a network of over 450 chambers of commerce and boards of trade, representing 200,000 businesses of all sizes in all sectors of the economy and in all regions, we are the largest business association in Canada, and the country's most influential." This site is an obvious choice when learning about the state of business in Canada, particularly how laws may affect you.
chamber.ca

Canadian Federation of Independent Businesses (CFIB)

The federation offers assistance and advocacy to small businesses across Canada.
cfib-fcei.ca/en

Canadian Government: Business information

A great resource with lots of information on just about everything you need to get started with your new business.
canada.ca/en/services/business.html

Canadian Government: Business number or Canada Revenue Agency program accounts

Information for "when you need a business number or Canada Revenue Agency program accounts."

canada.ca/en/revenue-agency/services/tax/businesses/topics/registering -your-business/you-need-a-business-number-a-program-account.html

Canadian Government: Canada's anti-spam legislation (CASL)

It's essential that you comply with these regulations, which will also help you protect your own business.

fightspam.gc.ca/eic/site/030.nsf/eng/00007.html

Canadian Government: Protecting your business

This page is an excellent resource for all sorts of protections, including against disasters, fraud, spam, environmental hazards, and much more.

canada.ca/en/services/business/protecting.html

Canadian Government: Registering your business with the government

Useful information if you have to register your business.

canada.ca/en/services/business/start/register-with-gov.html

Canadian Marketing Association

The CMA originated in the1960s, and now has over four hundred corporate members. It defines itself as an organization that "can help you grow your business, increase your team's marketing knowledge and safeguard your industry marketplace."

the-cma.org

Canadian Professional Sales Association

This is a sales networking membership site (currently with over 20,000 sales professionals as members) that offers training, webinars, templates and more. Available to individuals and teams.

cpsa.com

Canadian's Internet Business

Based in British Columbia, CIB describes itself as offering "tools, resources, legitimate opportunities, strategies and information from a Canadian perspective. The information provided will often be helpful to our friends in other countries who would like to do business with Canadians as well." They have a tab devoted to e-marketing, with pages that contain articles and links to dozens of valuable online resources.

canadiansinternet.com

Chief Content Officer

This is an online publication that offers a free subscription. It's geared toward content marketers and the tools they need, so go sign up!

contentmarketinginstitute.com/cco-digital/

Magazines Canada

This site is all about the Canadian magazine business, with an extensive directory of magazine addresses and websites, which is great for reaching out for advertising and marketing inquiries, as well as the possibility of stories about your business.

magazinescanada.ca

Newspapers Canada

From their LinkedIn profile: "The Canadian Community Newspapers Association (CCNA) and the Canadian Newspaper Association (CNA) are two separate organizations that partnered to form Newspapers Canada, creating one strong industry voice for newspapers in Canada." This is a great site for information on the Canadian newspaper industry, which will be very helpful when you're doing research for possible advertising and marketing.

nmc-mic.ca

Statistics Canada

This is a great place to start when you're looking for demographic and population data. There's a lot to explore here.

statcan.gc.ca

ABOUT THE AUTHOR

Tim Rayborn is a writer, educator, historian, musician, and researcher, with more than twenty years of professional experience. He is a prolific author, with a number of books and articles to his name, and more on the way. He has written on topics from the academic to the amusing to the appalling, including medieval and modern history, the arts (music, theater, and dance), food and wine, business, social studies, and works for business and government publications. He's also been a ghostwriter for various clients.

Based in the San Francisco Bay Area, Tim lived in England for seven years, studying for an M.A. and Ph.D. at the University of Leeds. He has a strong academic background but enjoys writing for general audiences.

He is also an acclaimed classical and world musician, having appeared on more than forty recordings, and he has toured and performed in the United States, Canada, Europe, North Africa, and Australia over the last twenty-five years. During that time, he has learned much about the business of arts and entertainment, and how to survive and thrive when traveling and working in intense environments.

For more, visit timrayborn.com.

INDEX

A

ability to learn from mistakes and failures, as part of the entrepreneur's mindset, 12
ability to think creatively, as part of the entrepreneur's mindset, 10
affiliate marketing, as type of internet marketing, 82
appendix, as part of business plan, 33, 35

B

balance sheet, 35, 118
being fearless, as part of the entrepreneur's mindset, 11
being open to change, as part of the entrepreneur's mindset, 10
blog, as type of internet marketing, 83–84
brick-and-mortar business, pros and cons of, 22–24
builder campaigns, 70
business loans, 34, 112, 146
business plan, 18, 32–35, 68, 119, 146

C

Canadian Revenue Agency (CRA), 105
cash-flow statement, 118
casual networks, 51
charities and community services, networking with, 54–55
collaborators, 18, 20, 126
college contacts, networking with, 54
company description, as part of business plan, 33
competitors, 15, 33, 44, 66, 69, 72, 108, 119, 127, 143, 144, 145
conferences, 43, 46, 126
consumer, as type of market, 91
contact networks, 51
content marketing, as type of internet marketing, 82
cooperative, as setup of business, 25, 27
corporation, as setup of business, 25–27
    incorporating provincially, 26
    incorporating federally, 27
cross-selling, 23, 124
crowdfunding, 113

D

desire to be challenged, as part of the entrepreneur's mindset, 10
desire to make things happen, as part of the entrepreneur's mindset, 9
driver campaigns, 70

E

e-commerce, 21
employees, 6, 19, 28, 32, 105, 119, 125, 131, 134, 140, 141–43, 144, 146
executive summary, as part of business plan, 32–33

F

family, networking with, 54
federal business number, 104
feeling fear, as part of the entrepreneur's mindset, 10
field trials, for market research, 64
financial outlook and forecast, as part of business plan, 34–35
focus groups, for market research, 63, 66, 92
former bosses and coworkers, networking with, 50, 54
friends, networking with, 53
funding needs, as part of business plan, 34

H

hiring employees, 106, 117, 122, 133, 135, 136, 137, 145

I

ideas, definition of, 17
income statement, 118
industrial, as type of market, 91
influencers, as type of internet marketing, 84
Instagram, marketing on, 87–88
intellectual assets, 107–8
intellectual property, 107–9, 128
interests, as source of business ideas, 13–14
interviews, for market research, 63
interviews, of potential employees, 137–40
investors, 18, 19, 32, 35, 68, 69, 91, 149
irritations, as source of business ideas, 14

J

joint-venture marketing, 102

K

keywords, for SEO, 74, 84, 87

L

liability insurance, 111
licensing, 33, 128–30
LinkedIn, networking on, 56–57

M

magazines, marketing with, 80–81
management and organization summary, as part of business plan, 34
market analysis, as part of business plan, 33
marketing and sales strategy, as part of business plan, 34
marketing plan, 68–70, 149
marketing, definition of, 60

N

networking, 29, 43–44, 49, 51, 53, 54, 56, 86, 134, 135, 152
never being satisfied, as part of the entrepreneur's mindset, 11
newsletter, as type of internet marketing, 83
newspapers, marketing with, 79–80
nondisclosure agreements, 107, 109, 142–43

O

offering discounts, as a way to close a sale, 98, 99
online business, pros and cons of, 20–22
opportunities, definition of, 17–18

P

paid advertising, as type of internet marketing, 84–85
partners, 29–31
partnership, as setup of business, 25–26
    general partnership, as setup of business, 25–26
    limited partnership, as setup of business, 26
    limited liability partnership (LLP), as setup of business, 26
patents, 33, 35, 108
Pinterest, marketing on, 89
possibilities, as type of potential customer, 92
primary research, for market research, 62–63
products and services that you offer, as part of business plan, 33
professional associations, 52, 151
property insurance, 110
prospects, as type of potential customer, 92
psychographics, 66

R

radio, marketing with, 76–77
recruiters, 136

rent, of a physical business location, 23
repeat customers, 23, 100, 118, 124, 145
reseller, as type of market, 91

S

schedules, for managing business-related tasks, 21, 36, 38, 39, 40
search engine optimization (SEO), 21, 74, 84, 144
secondary research, for market research, 62
seeing other points of view, as part of the entrepreneur's mindset, 11–12
self-employment, 15, 40, 42
self-financing, 112
Snapchat, marketing on, 88–89
Social Insurance Number, 141
social media analytics, 66
social proof, 22, 49, 74, 84
sole proprietorship, as setup of business, 25, 27, 34, 115
spam, 58, 111, 152
Strengths, Weakness, Opportunities, and Threats (SWOT) analysis, 68
surveys, for market research, 63

T

talents, as source of business ideas, 14
target market, 14, 15, 16, 33, 61, 62, 63, 65, 66, 72, 77, 83, 93, 97, 124, 125, 126
taxes, 6, 25, 28, 115, 116, 122
television, marketing with, 77–78
time-sensitive offers, as a way to close a sale, 98
trade shows, 126, 127
trademarks, 107, 108

V

venture capital, 34, 113

W

willingness to listen and learn, as part of the entrepreneur's mindset, 11
willingness to take action, as part of the entrepreneur's mindset, 9
word-of-mouth referrals, 22, 51, 92

Y

YouTube, marketing on, 86–87

PUBLISHING PRACTICAL & CREATIVE NONFICTION

Whalen Book Works is a small, independent book publishing company based in Kennebunkport, Maine, that combines top-notch design, unique formats, and fresh content to create truly innovative gift books.

Our unconventional approach to bookmaking is a close-knit, creative, and collaborative process among authors, artists, designers, editors, and booksellers. We publish a small, carefully curated list each season, and we take the time to make each book exactly what it needs to be.

We believe in giving back. That's why we plant one tree for every ten books sold. Your purchase supports a tree in the Rocky Mountain National Park.

Visit us at **WHALENBOOKS.COM**
or write to us at
68 North Street, Kennebunkport, ME 04046

TAKE YOUR CAREER TO THE NEXT LEVEL!

OTHER TITLES IN THE SERIES INCLUDE:

Become a Manager,
ISBN 978-1-951511-08-1,
$11.95 US / $16.95 CAN

Business Etiquette,
ISBN 978-1-951511-09-8,
$11.95 US / $16.95 CAN

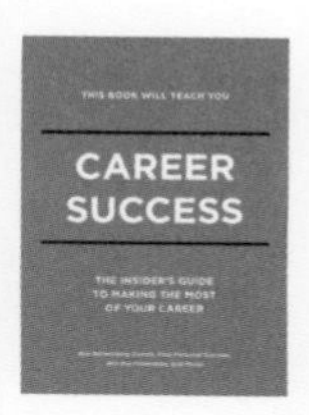

Career Success,
ISBN 978-1-951511-14-2,
$11.95 US / $16.95 CAN

Essential Sales Strategies,
ISBN 978-1-951511-12-8,
$11.95 US / $16.95 CAN

Marketing Fundamentals,
ISBN 978-1-951511-13-5,
$11.95 US / $16.95 CAN

Own Your Time,
ISBN 978-1-951511-10-4,
$11.95 US / $16.95 CAN

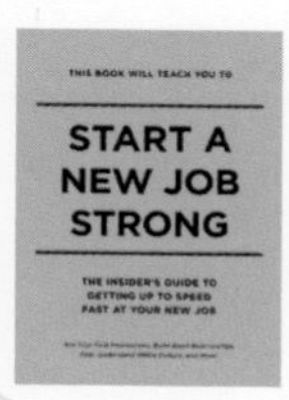

Start a New Job Strong,
ISBN 978-1-951511-07-4,
$11.95 US / $16.95 CAN